Making the Best of a Bad Decision

How to put your regrets behind you, embrace grace, and move toward a better future

ERWIN W. LUTZER

Tyndale House Publishers, Inc.
Carol Stream, Illinois

Visit Tyndale's exciting website at www.tyndale.com.

TYNDALE and Tyndale's quill logo are registered trademarks of Tyndale House Publishers, Inc.

Making the Best of a Bad Decision: How to Put Your Regrets behind You, Embrace Grace, and Move toward a Better Future

Copyright © 2011 by Erwin W. Lutzer. All rights reserved.

Cover photo of glass copyright © Andrew Pini/Photolibrary. All rights reserved.

Cover photo of lemon copyright © FoodCollection/Photolibrary. All rights reserved.

Designed by Ron Kaufmann

Unless otherwise indicated, Scripture quotations are taken from the Holy Bible, *New International Version,*® *NIV.*® Copyright © 1973, 1978, 1984, 2010 by Biblica, Inc.™ Used by permission of Zondervan. All rights reserved worldwide. www.zondervan.com.

Scripture quotations marked ESV are taken from *The Holy Bible*, English Standard Version® (ESV®), copyright © 2001 by Crossway Bibles, a publishing ministry of Good News Publishers. Used by permission. All rights reserved.

Scripture quotations marked NASB are taken from the New American Standard Bible,® copyright © 1960, 1962, 1963, 1968, 1971, 1972, 1973, 1975, 1977, 1995 by The Lockman Foundation. Used by permission.

Scripture quotations marked PHI are taken from *The New Testament in Modern English* by J. B. Phillips, copyright © J. B. Phillips, 1958, 1959, 1960, 1972. All rights reserved.

Library of Congress Cataloging-in-Publication Data

Lutzer, Erwin W.
   Making the best of a bad decision : how to put your regrets behind you, embrace grace, and move toward a better future / Erwin Lutzer.
      p. cm.
   Includes bibliographical references.
   ISBN 978-1-4143-1143-2 (sc)
   1. Decision making—Religious aspects—Christianity. 2. Choice (Psychology)—Religious aspects—Christianity. 3. Adjustment (Psychology)—Religious aspects—Christianity. 4. Discernment (Christian theology) 5. Providence and government of God—Christianity. 6. Grace (Theology) 7. Encouragement—Religious aspects—Christianity. I. Title.
   BV4509.5.L88 2011
   248.8'6—dc22   2011011326

Printed in the United States of America

17   16   15   14   13   12   11
 7   6   5   4   3   2   1

Contents

SO YOU'VE MADE A BAD DECISION . . .

You're in good company!

Smart people can make foolish decisions!

We've all known brilliant people who chose a dead-end career, married an incompatible mate, or were seduced by a get-rich-quick scheme. We've all made decisions we would rather forget, but sometimes we can't forget them because the consequences keep piling up.

The sum of our lives equals the sum of our decisions. Our character is best revealed by the decisions we've made and the impact of those decisions on ourselves and others. Who we *are* will determine what we decide to *do*—that is, our character will dictate the kind of decisions we make.

We are free to make our choices, but we are not free to choose the consequences. Even more sobering is this: One bad choice can result in a lifetime of heartache and regret. One act of immorality, one drunken-driving episode, one hasty marriage—these and countless other foolish choices can alter the direction and trajectory of our lives for the worse. And having begun on the wrong road, you might find it difficult (and sometimes seemingly impossible) to turn around.

We are free to make our choices, but we are not free to choose the consequences.

The decisions you've made in the past have affected where you are today on the journey of life. Likewise, the decisions you make today will to some extent determine your future. Wise choices can transform the bad decisions of the past into a foundation for a more productive life and ministry—starting right now.

Making good decisions under challenging circumstances is difficult, but not impossible. The Old Testament story about a young man named Joseph, who made a series of good choices despite being grossly betrayed by his jealous brothers, is a good example. Joseph turned away from the seductive advances of his boss's wife, endured several years of wrongful imprisonment as a result, and later refused to retaliate against his brothers when he had the chance. He chose humility over pride and forgiveness over bitterness. We honor him today because his wise choices had positive consequences far beyond his imagination.

Like Joseph, we wake up every morning with decisions to make about the day. We will choose either the best path or a

ERWIN W. LUTZER

lesser one, but when the day is over, we never can return to where we started. Over time, the decisions we make—whether small or large—will become the legacy we leave behind.

I have a friend who bought some highly recommended mining stock and encouraged others to do the same. Every indication was that the company was poised for growth—unusual growth. But an explosion in a mine ended the upswing and investors lost about 80 percent of their money. Obviously, my friend had no legal obligation to help those to whom he had recommended the stock, but he felt he had a *moral* obligation to them. He decided to sell his house to raise the cash to restore their investments. After all, he reasoned, his friends had lost money because of his recommendation. Think of how that man and his wife will be remembered!

Making good decisions under challenging circumstances is difficult, but not impossible.

This book is about making the best of our bad decisions. It is written with the firm belief that God takes what we sometimes call our "second best" decisions and turns them into what we can call his "first best" decisions, if only we will invite him to walk alongside us. When we find ourselves on a wrong road, God is able to bring us to an intersection where we can choose a new path that will lead us to something better. It's our failure to see God in the midst of our missteps that keeps us stumbling from one bad decision to another. God specializes in redirecting those who desire a better path.

In the pages that follow, you will inevitably arrive at a fork in the road—confronted by yet another decision: Will you continue to be defined by your bad decisions, or will you look beyond them to God, who can take what you give him and turn it into something productive and eternal? You can choose a life of prolonged regret or a life of optimism and fulfillment. It's your call.

Failure to see God in the midst of our missteps keeps us stumbling from one bad decision to another.

In this book, you will meet people who have made terrible decisions: criminals, sex addicts, and people who have destroyed their marriages and their families through immorality or some other form of self-absorption. You'll meet people who have made foolish promises; and others who have lost their livelihood through gambling or bad investments. In other words, if you've chosen the wrong path and are living with the consequences, you'll find yourself somewhere in these pages.

But this is ultimately a book of *hope*. The fact that you are alive is proof that there are still some wise decisions you can make! No matter how many wrong paths you've already walked, there is still a right one you can choose just up ahead. God is bigger than your foolishness; bigger than the mistakes you've made; bigger than your sins; and bigger than the messes you've left along the road you've chosen up till now.

God is bigger than the mistakes you've made.

My prayer is to offer you *encouragement*, despite all the choices you now wish had been different. I invite you to join me on a journey of expectation and hope. Along the way, we'll learn how God's forgiveness and power are able make a beautiful painting from the blotches we hand him.

1

THE WORST DECISION EVER MADE

Thankfully, it wasn't yours

What, in your opinion, was the worst decision ever made? No matter how badly you think you have blown it, I can assure you that others have made worse decisions. God was there to redeem their poor choices and set them on a different path, so we can be sure he is there for us when we take a wrong turn on the road of life.

Paradise Lost

In the Bible, we're told about a couple who made the worst decision of all time. Surrounded by the most perfect environment, they chose a path with incredibly far-reaching consequences. In fact, their decision has affected every generation since theirs, right up to today. No other decision has so negatively affected so many people for so long a time—for eternity, to be exact. Of course, at the moment of truth, they didn't know that their decision would boomerang and give birth to all kinds of evil: violence, natural disasters, and even death. Yes, Adam and Eve win the prize for the worst decision ever made. But if we can recognize that God was both able and willing to make the best of their self-made tragedy, we can be confident that he stands ready to help us, too.

The Opportunities They Had

Visualize Adam and Eve in Paradise. They enjoyed a perfect environment, with no unfulfilled needs. They lived in a beautiful garden, surrounded by God's masterful handiwork, and their five senses were undiminished and uncorrupted. Were they hungry? There were many trees in the Garden from which they could freely eat. And if they had wanted something they didn't already have, they could've asked God, and I'm sure he would have created it for them.

Eve had no insecurities. She not only lived in a perfect environment, but she also had a perfect husband! I'm sure Adam faithfully carried out the garbage and helped with the dinner dishes. No doubt he was sensitive, caring, romantic, and all those other things so rightly prized by women. Eve didn't have to worry about the woman next door becoming too friendly with Adam. She didn't have to compete with supermodels and actresses on

Adam and Eve win the prize for the worst decision ever made.

every magazine cover. And she didn't have to lie awake at night wondering whether she had married the right man!

Adam and Eve also had the advantage of direct access to God. They walked with him in the cool of the day, evidently enjoying discussions and very likely having their questions answered. But one day they made a choice that ended their evening walks with the Almighty. Standing together by the one tree in the Garden they'd been told not to eat from, Adam and Eve made a decision that contaminated their relationship with God and with each other. In effect, by a single bite of a forbidden fruit, they became God's enemies, and their own beautiful relationship turned sour.

Eve didn't lie awake at night wondering whether she had married the right man!

Now, if you ask why this couple chose to disobey God, even though they were in a perfect environment and had everything they wanted and needed, there's no good answer. The Bible doesn't give us a full explanation. What we do know is that, in our own day and age, people make bad decisions all the time, despite privileged circumstances and loving families. Like Adam and Eve, we often choose to do what we think is best for ourselves, and we disregard the warnings and wisdom of others, including God.

The Decision They Made

God's command was clear: "You are free to eat from any tree in the garden; but you must not eat from the tree of the knowledge of good and evil, for when you eat from it you will certainly die" (Genesis 2:16-17).

When Satan, in the guise of a serpent, approached Eve, he focused—as he so often does—on the *one thing* that God had placed off limits. He diverted Eve's attention from all the goodness surrounding her and Adam—the many trees from which they were free to eat—and called into question God's wisdom and love. He tricked Eve into thinking she could do better by disregarding God's clear command.

Adam, of course, doesn't get a free pass here. He stood by while Eve was tempted and then joined in her bad decision to eat the forbidden fruit. And so they sinned, even while surrounded by innumerable blessings.

Maybe your own story is like that. Maybe you were brought up in a stable home, with loving parents and wonderful opportunities. Yet the allure of doing your own thing distracted you from what you knew was best. Maybe you followed your desires and ignored your best instincts.

Let's look more closely at what drew Adam and Eve off track. It all began when Eve elevated her own desires above God's wisdom. The tree was desirable—it was pleasant to the eyes, and it appeared as if it would make her wise. At the moment of decision, that meant more to her than what God had said. She

> **Satan tricked Eve into thinking she could do better by disregarding God's clear command.**

was deceived by her senses, and that gave her the courage to ignore God's word. In essence what the serpent said to her was, "Eve, *feel*, don't *think*. It looks good—do it! It if feels good, how can it be bad?"

Of course, our emotions don't always mislead us, but like Adam and Eve we are often tempted to take the path of least resistance when pursuing something we desire. The decisions we make can seem so simple, and yet the consequences can be devastating. God had warned Adam and Eve that they

We are often tempted to take the path of least resistance when pursuing something we desire.

would die if they ate the wrong fruit, but at that point they didn't even know what death was! There was no example of death in Paradise. Perhaps Eve was curious: "I wonder what death really is? Maybe death will be a wonderful experience, better than life itself." Then there was the added promise that, if they ate, they would be "like God, knowing good and evil" (Genesis 3:5).

A Window into Our Hearts

Our minds can justify anything that our hearts really want to do. Whether we like to admit it or not, we are driven by our desires. We may think we make decisions based on rational considerations, but we are much more influenced by our passions and our appetites. Because we have to live with our consciences, we carefully rationalize what we really want to do—and continue to rationalize after we've done it. Our minds become enslaved to whatever our desires demand. We tell ourselves, *Nobody's perfect, but I'm basically a good person. Besides, it isn't my fault things turned out the way they did.*

Moments after Adam and Eve sinned, the finger-pointing began. Adam passed the blame to God and to Eve, and she passed it on to the serpent. Adam and Eve were incapable of seeing themselves as they really were, and so are we. Our rationalizations become deep and lasting, and we become entrenched until we are shaken awake by a moment of reality—often it takes a crisis to awaken the conscience. You've heard it said that most people change only when they see the light, but it's more accurate to say that we change only when we *feel the heat*!

We carefully rationalize what we really want to do— and continue to rationalize after we've done it.

Eve gave birth to a son and they named him Cain. As Eve nursed him, she had no idea the consequences of sin that awaited their little family. When a second son was born, they named him Abel. He grew to be a godly young man who learned to bring the right kind of offering—a blood sacrifice—to God. Cain, the firstborn, also brought an offering, one from the fruit of the ground. But God rejected his offering even as he accepted Abel's. Jealousy now took root in Cain's heart, and in a fit of rage he killed his brother. Another terrible decision. Thus the long and sordid history of dysfunctional families began.

No Return to Paradise

Before Adam and Eve sinned, they were naked but not ashamed. Imagine having a relationship with God, and with other people, without shame or guilt getting in the way. Imagine if your thoughts were so pure, so holy, that you would have no shame even if your most private musings were known to your spouse, your children, your parents, and your friends. Imagine the freedom this would bring to your relationships: no anger, lust, pride, or selfishness.

Despite their deep regret, Adam and Eve could not return to Paradise. God set up a barrier that forced them to stay away from the home they once enjoyed. Every morning when they awoke outside of Eden, they regretfully remembered that things were not as they once had been. Their innocence could not be restored; no amount of tears would grant them the privilege of spending so much as a night in the idyllic surroundings they had once enjoyed.

Sound familiar?

Imagine having a relationship with God, and with other people, without shame or guilt getting in the way.

The young couple who have surrendered to temptation and slept together can never have their virginity restored. The man who has foolishly gambled away his savings or squandered it on a get-rich-quick scheme cannot recover what he has lost. The woman who has married against her parents' advice and now regrets having to live with an indifferent husband cannot retrace her steps and back out of her vows.

Ever since the days of Adam and Eve, we have been deceived by the attractiveness of sin just like they were. In fact, we're often eager to believe the lies that tell us we can do whatever our sinful desires dictate. It's as if we long to be deceived. We live with regrets, just as they did, and we wish we could undo our foolish decisions, but all those bad decisions create a barrier that keeps us from ever going back to the way things were.

But even as the door to Paradise was closing to Adam and Eve (and to us), the door of hope swung wide open. God assures us that something good can still be made from the pieces of our broken lives.

Hope amid Regret and Loss

After Adam and Eve sinned, they hid themselves among the trees of the Garden. They who had felt no shame were now crushed by its powerful effects. The trees that had once been a pleasant backdrop to fellowship with their Creator now became a wall to hide themselves from him and from one another. From then on, much psychological energy and ingenuity would be expended to keep hiding. Adam and Eve had reason to feel ashamed.

We're often eager to believe the lies that tell us we can do whatever our sinful desires dictate.

Shame is a powerful emotion. I'm told that in Japan, if a man is fired from his job, he often will not tell his family; and if he continues to be out of work, he will not go home. This has contributed to the rise of a street culture in Japanese cities. Suicide is on the rise. We so desire acceptance that we will be emotionally destroyed if we don't get it.

Albert Camus, in *The Fall*, writes, "Each of us insists on being innocent at all cost, even if he has to accuse the whole human race and heaven itself."[1] Some people, filled with narcissistic obsessions, are psychologically incapable of taking responsibility for anything, no matter how unjust, corrupt, or abusive their behavior. They appear incapable of entering into the pain of others, but interpret such misfortunes only in relationship to themselves. They will go to their graves without uttering the words, "I have sinned" or "I'm sorry."

We so desire acceptance that we will be emotionally destroyed if we don't get it.

Adam and Eve both admitted to what they had done, but they wouldn't take responsibility for it. As the saying goes, the man blamed the woman, the woman blamed the serpent, and the serpent didn't have a leg to stand on! We have clearly followed in their footsteps, stoutly resisting our own responsibility; blaming others; shaping the facts to protect our selfish egos; and if necessary, destroying those around us in order to preserve our own sense of self-worth.

After the Fall, Adam and Eve weren't trying to find their way back to God; they simply hid from him. It was God who initiated the search (as he always does), walking in the Garden and

Adam and Eve weren't trying to find their way back to God; they simply hid from him.

calling out to the disgraced couple. If anything, they sought to become their own gods, so that they wouldn't have to be exposed to the holiness of the one whom they had wronged. But thankfully, the true God wouldn't let them go. His search among the trees of the Garden was the beginning of their redemption—and ours.

Into the middle of this mess, God came to inject a healthy dose of grace. He cursed the serpent, to be sure, but in doing so he gave a wonderful promise of hope to humanity. In *Paradise Lost,* John Milton speaks of it as "the fortunate fall," because when we are brought back to God there is glory in our restoration. Sin has no glory, but reconciliation does.

The Promise

When God confronted Adam and Eve about their sin, he also spoke to the serpent: "I will put enmity between you and the woman, and between your offspring and hers; he will crush your head, and you will strike his heel" (Genesis 3:15).

What does this promise mean?

A Redeemer committed to rescuing humanity from their sin and folly was on his way! The woman's offspring—a reference to Jesus Christ—would crush the head of the serpent, even as the serpent would bite him on the heel. In other words, the heel of the Redeemer would grind the head of the serpent into the dust. The Redeemer would win the battle decisively. No contest.

This story is familiar to anyone who has studied the Bible, but I recount it here because it is central to God's plan for making the best of our bad decisions. Bad decisions cannot be undone, but they can be redeemed. And Jesus Christ is the key.

Centuries later, when Jesus died on the cross, the serpent deceived himself by thinking, *Now that I've killed him, I've destroyed my opposition!* But three days later, Jesus rose from the grave; and a few weeks later, he went to heaven in undisputed triumph. His wound was light

Bad decisions cannot be undone, but they can be redeemed.

and temporary; the serpent's wound was fatal, decisive, and permanent. It's in the power of the Redeemer that we're able to make the best of our bad decisions.

"Through your faith in the working of God, . . . [he] made you alive with Christ. He forgave us all our sins, having canceled the charge of our legal indebtedness, which stood against us and condemned us; he has taken it away, nailing it to the cross. And having disarmed the powers and authorities, he made a public spectacle of them, triumphing over them by the cross" (Colossians 2:12-15). Jesus disarmed Satan, exposing the devil as a shimmering fraud.

The Covering

After they sinned, Adam and Eve clothed themselves with fig leaves. No doubt if they'd had enough of them, they might have been able to make dresses and shirts. But even though the fig leaves enabled them to hide from one another, their self-styled clothing did not hide them from God. Fig leaves might make a dress, but they soon wither. God knew they needed a more permanent covering; an expensive covering that only he could supply.

"The LORD God made garments of skin for Adam and his wife and clothed them" (Genesis 3:21). Where did God get the skins? Evidently, he killed one of the animals of the field. With this sacrificial provision, God began teaching a basic principle: Blood must be shed for the forgiveness and covering of our sin. *There could be no cheap covering for sin.*

God dressed Adam and Eve so that their fellowship with him could be restored and their sin and shame covered. Those animal skins had no intrinsic value, but they symbolized what would become clear later: that sin must be not only forgiven but covered. Throughout history, many animals were sacrificed, pointing to the future coming of Jesus, "the Lamb of God, who takes away the sin of the world" (John 1:29).

Withering fig leaves wouldn't do. Centuries after Adam and Eve, God himself had to suffer on the cross so that we might be forgiven. His forgiveness, though costly to him, is given freely to us. "God made him who had no sin to be sin for us, so that in him we might become the righteousness of God" (2 Corinthians 5:21). That truth doesn't change just because we make some bad decisions.

> **God began teaching a basic principle: Blood must be shed for the forgiveness and covering of our sin.**

What God Does with Our Sin

Many people today have a neurotic preoccupation with their sin. Sometimes they confess their sins to one another, which brings them temporary relief. Most often, they resolve to do better, trying to find within themselves a reason why God should forgive them. Even when they confess their sins to God, there is no permanent relief from the feeling that they have messed up and are condemned to mess up again in the future.

The first step toward breaking out of this trap is to understand that nothing within us merits God's forgiveness. Minimizing our sin does not make us worthy before God; magnifying our sin does not give us reason to think we are beyond forgiveness. *Forgiveness and reconciliation with God are given freely, apart from what we have done or who we are.*

Forgiveness and reconciliation with God are given freely, apart from what we have done or who we are.

We are pardoned because of the death of another—the promised Redeemer sent by God. We have been justified by his blood (Romans 5:9); we have our consciences cleansed by his blood (Hebrews 9:14); and the serpent—our accuser—has been defeated by his blood (Revelation 12:11). The work of Christ is the one and only basis of our forgiveness. Neither our goodness nor our badness affects this objective fact.

God provides something better and more permanent than fig leaves or the skins of animals to cover our guilt and shame. We are credited with the righteousness of Jesus Christ. David, whose sins of adultery and murder are well known, writes, "How blessed is he whose transgression is forgiven, whose sin is covered!" (Psalm 32:1, NASB). God himself puts it this way: "I have swept away your offenses like a cloud, your sins like the morning mist" (Isaiah 44:22).

God provides something better and more permanent than fig leaves or the skins of animals to cover our guilt and shame.

A man who wrote me from prison confessed to raping four women; he asked if he, too, could be forgiven. In my response, I used the following analogy: Imagine two roads; one is clean and well traveled, the other has deep ruts that veer off into the ditch. When a blanket of snow comes, it covers each one equally. Just so, our sins—big or small—are equally covered by God. "'Come now, let us settle the matter,' says the LORD. 'Though your sins are like scarlet, they shall be as white as snow; though they are red as crimson, they shall be like wool'" (Isaiah 1:18).

Yes, even horrendous crimes can be forgiven by God; the worst evil can be covered.

The God of the Second Chance

Read this story of redemption.

A minister who committed immorality and had to resign in disgrace told me, "Just think of peeling an onion, and as you do, layer after layer comes off, but there is nothing in the center. There was nothing left, just me and God. Because of shame, I retreated from every friend who ever knew me. I was despised, spoken about—and I deserved whatever was said about me. I wondered how I could keep getting up every morning and put one foot ahead of another."

As we drove together in his car, he put a CD in the stereo and wept as we heard these words:

Calvary covers it all,
My past with its sin and stain [read, shame];
My guilt and despair
Jesus took on Him there,
And Calvary covers it all.[2]

Calvary meant there was a new beginning available for him. Much had been lost that could never be regained, but not all was lost. He had been restored to fellowship with God and was beginning to form new friendships. Small blessings along his path reminded him that God had not cast him aside. And as time rolled on, more and more grace was there for him.

Even horrendous crimes can be forgiven by God; the worst evil can be covered.

You say, "But nothing will ever be the same for him again." That is true; it won't. His sin destroyed his marriage and affected his children. But neither was life the same for Adam and Eve; yet God gave them garments to wear—restoring their relationship with him through sacrifice. And he does the same for us. All we can do is give him the broken pieces of our bad decisions and trust him to heal our souls.

Yes, God had to kill animals to give Adam and Eve proper clothing. And Jesus had to be killed so that our sin might be properly covered. Remember, the purpose of the Cross is to repair the irreparable; it is God's answer when it seems that the fragments of our lives can never be put back together. That's why we read in Romans 10:11 that those who put their trust in God will never be put to shame—they can never be finally and wholly destroyed.

In Eden, God became God of the second chance.

More Sin, More Grace

Adam and Eve were the first but obviously not the last people who took a wrong turn on the road of life. Thanks to them, we're all born on the wrong road and stand in need of God's grace.

Much had been lost that could never be regained, but not all was lost.

Fortunately, the greater our sin, the greater God's grace toward us. "Where sin increased, grace increased all the more, so that, just as sin reigned in death, so also grace might reign through righteousness to bring eternal life through Jesus Christ our Lord" (Romans 5:20-21). God promises to turn curses into blessings and failures into stepping-stones.

Though Adam and Eve were properly clothed and their fellowship with God restored, the cruel consequences of their sin have continued throughout history. We all bear the marks of the Fall. Nevertheless, God picked them up where they were and set them on a new journey. They would no longer walk with God in the Garden, but they—and their descendants—would still maintain fellowship with him because their sin was covered. The effect of their bad decision would not be reversed, but they could continue to serve God by working the soil and populating the earth. *The serpent could not stop God from granting forgiveness and grace.*

In the wake of Adam and Eve's bad decision, sin and grace now always exist together. With curses there are blessings; with crimes there is also mercy. There is hatred, but also love; and despair is offset by hope.

Thanks to Adam and Eve, we're all born on the wrong road and stand in need of God's grace.

Although this grace is offered to everyone, however, it is not enjoyed by everyone. Grace abounds to those who have the humility to receive it. Those who cling to their fig leaves—that is, their own goodness—will continue to be frustrated, making decisions that appear right but always lead to a dead end. They might enjoy their temporal successes, but in the end they will find nothing to take with them into the life beyond.

Jesus told a story about two men, both of whom believed in grace—yet only one experienced the miracle of God's acceptance; the other, good man though he was, was rejected.

The story, from the Gospel of Luke, is a familiar one in which an upstanding Pharisee and a despised tax collector went into the Temple to pray. The Pharisee prayed,

Grace abounds to those who have the humility to receive it.

"God, I thank You that I am not like other people: swindlers, unjust, adulterers, or even like this tax collector. I fast twice a week; I pay tithes of all that I get" (Luke 18:11-12, NASB).

If we think he was bragging, let's remember that he believed in grace. In thanking God that he was not like other men, he was, in effect, saying, "There, but for the grace of God, go I." He knew that his good works were done because of God's goodness. If he was better than others, God deserved the credit.

In contrast, the tax collector was so overwhelmed by his sin that he would not even lift his face to heaven, but pounded his chest and said, "God, be merciful to me, the sinner!" (Luke 18:13, NASB).

Referring to the tax collector, Jesus added, "I tell you, this man went to his house justified rather than the other; for everyone who exalts himself will be humbled, but he who humbles himself will be exalted" (Luke 18:14, NASB).

Yes, both men believed in God's grace. The self-righteous Pharisee thought that God's grace was needed only to do good deeds. God's grace, he thought, helps us do better. The tax gatherer knew that if he was to be saved, it would take a miracle that only God could do. He didn't just need help; he needed the gift of forgiveness, the gift of reconciliation. Only God could do what needed to be done.

The crushing experience of having to admit total helplessness apart from God's grace is not easy for anyone.

Was it difficult for this sinner, this tax gatherer, to receive grace? Depends. On the one hand, no, for he was relieved to discover that there was grace for the needy. On the other hand, the grace of God was very difficult to accept. The crushing experience of having to admit total helplessness apart from God's grace is not easy for anyone. And that is why the road that leads to life is narrow and only a few find it (Matthew 7:14).

No wonder John Newton, a former slave trader who understood grace, knew that neither our life on earth nor our stay in heaven will exhaust our wonder at God's provision.

> *When we've been there ten thousand years,*
> *Bright shining as the sun,*
> *We've no less days to sing God's praise*
> *Than when we'd first begun.*[3]

When sin entered the world, grace was there to meet it. For those who will accept it, grace is available to restore our broken fellowship with our Creator and to redeem even the worst of our bad decisions.

A Prayer

God, I thank you that there is more grace in your heart than there is sin in my past. Although I have made my share of bad decisions, I know that you can forgive my past and cover my sin so that it will no longer separate me from your fellowship and holiness.

Thank you that Jesus died in my place so that I can inherit his righteousness. I bring nothing but my great need; I count on your grace to give me what I don't have.

2

WHEN YOU'VE CHOSEN SECOND BEST

*Trusting God while traveling
on the wrong path*

We have all made our share of bad decisions. Sometimes it's because we've acted contrary to our better judgment, and sometimes because we simply did not have all the facts. We've all had to choose blindly at times, with a hunch that our decision might not be wise, but convinced we can deal with the consequences. Some of these decisions were of little consequence; others greatly affected our lives and the lives of those around us.

I saw a report the other day of a dozen cars that were sidelined on a Chicago expressway after they hit a deep pothole. Truth is, we often don't see the potholes along our paths until we find ourselves in the ditch. Unfortunately, we see our mistakes more clearly in the rearview mirror as we travel life's road, and we somehow fail to anticipate the dangers we are about to encounter. A single decision that appears inconsequential can change the entire direction of our lives. If only we were wiser, we wouldn't be where we are today, wondering whether we'll ever get back on the expressway.

We often don't see the potholes along our paths until we find ourselves in the ditch.

Often we make bad decisions that are not necessarily sinful; they are simply errors of judgment—or at least we perceive them as errors in judgment, only to find out later that these choices might have been best after all. But there are other times when we knowingly do wrong; we know what God expects, but we choose our own path anyway.

On a recent airplane trip, the young woman seated next to me told me her story. She was pregnant, she said, after dating her boyfriend for about six months. He was willing to marry her, but she wasn't sure that she wanted to marry him.

Sometimes we know what God expects, but we choose our own path anyway.

"I want to be married for all the right reasons, not because we have to, so I'm taking the weekend off to discuss this with my sister."

She asked my opinion and I gave it to her, although I told her she might be better served by listening to the advice of someone who knew her and the father of the child. I warned her that my observation has been that "have to" marriages usually don't do well; most end in divorce. Perhaps she and her boyfriend would make it long term, but marriage is hard work under the best of conditions.

If she married, she said, she'd have to settle for "second best." Faced with the realities of her situation, there was no obvious choice; one way or another, her future was "ruined."

Although I understood why she felt the way she did, I assured her that God is greater than the messes we create for ourselves and for others. Many children conceived out of wedlock have become great men and women, serving God with distinction—the great scholar Erasmus, the Christian martyr Felix Manz, and the famous singer Ethel Waters, to name just a few. I encouraged her

God is greater than the messes we create for ourselves and for others.

to keep her baby, but also to get in touch with her church and pastor so that she would have proper support and counsel going forward.

What this young woman was asking is, How can I make the best of an unwise or hasty decision that had unintended consequences? What happens when you can't just pull yourself up by your bootstraps and get back on track, but instead feel as if you must spend the rest of your life in the ditch while others pass you by on the main road? Can you have the assurance that God will bless you even if your marriage has gone sour, or you've had a child out of wedlock, had an abortion, committed a crime, or made an investment decision that has left you in financial ruin?

Making bad choices can become a downward spiral. If you were brought up in a home where you were constantly told that you would be a failure, you will have a strong tendency

Making bad choices can become a downward spiral.

to live out that perception. You'll think that failure is written on your forehead; in fact, you might fear success. A woman I met said that whenever she applied for work, something within her said, *You won't get this job; and even if you did, you'd fail.* More people than we realize not only fear success, but actually plan to fail. One person I know flits from job to job about every six months or a year. He lives with the fear that he just might succeed. His father was an alcoholic, and there were no role models of success in his family. Even as a Christian, he seemingly cannot embrace God's help to break the cycle of failure in his family. He's afraid of what God might want him to do; he fears that if he were to pursue success, God would see to it that he failed.

Other people respond to a negative home life by doing everything they can to prove their parents wrong. But that can lead to bad decisions as well. "Nothing would please my

Other people respond to a negative home life by doing everything they can to prove their parents wrong.

mother more than if I were to fail," a young man told me. But he had "disappointed" her by becoming financially successful, though at a great price. Like others who think they need to prove themselves, he became a workaholic and overcompensated for his insecurity by surrounding himself with the trappings of material success.

In an interview, former supermodel Janice Dickinson said she was motivated to be a model because she constantly heard the voice of her father ringing in her ears: "You are ugly and could never be a model." She proved him wrong, but at a price. While ascending in her career, she lived a life of immorality and drug abuse.

One bad decision opens the door to other bad decisions, and the vicious cycle spins out of control until, in desperation, people are driven to seek help. But getting back on the right path is often difficult when much of your life is already spent. The good news, however, is that it is *still possible*. No matter what happened yesterday, tomorrow can be different.

Even as we round the next corner of a collapsing career, a failed investment, or a difficult marriage, God is waiting to meet us. We might never get back to where we were when we got off track, but God can blaze a new trail for us to make the best of our bad decisions. He is even able to take our "second best" and turn it into his "first best" if we give him the broken pieces.

Getting back on the right path is often difficult when much of your life is already spent.

There is always one right choice we can still make: surrendering our lives and everything we have to God.

God and Your Second Best

As we read the Bible, we can often apply the experiences of the nation of Israel to our own lives. For example, in one startling incident from the book of Exodus we see the ugliness of sin, how other people's bad decisions can affect us as much as our own, and how God's compassion can create a pathway of redemption even when we or someone close to us has chosen "second best."

The Paralysis of Fear

After the nation of Israel escaped from Egypt, they traveled across the wilderness to the brink of the Promised Land. For two full years, they had been told how wonderful this new land would be, that it was abundantly fruitful and could sustain livestock. Over and over, they heard the land described as "flowing with milk and honey." And now they were about to enter and take possession of it. Everyone—all two million people, young and old—was looking forward to leaving the desert behind in exchange for this prosperous new real estate that God had promised.

Then they made a tragic decision. When the twelve spies who had been sent to scout the land returned, only two of them, Joshua and Caleb, brought an optimistic report. The other ten gave in to their fears and counseled safety and immediate security. They said, "We can't attack those people; they are stronger than we are" (Numbers 13:31). Even though Joshua and Caleb tried to persuade the people that God would give them the victory, the congregation voted with the majority of spies.

> **God's compassion can create a pathway of redemption even when we've chosen "second best."**

Don't miss the bottom line: God had promised the people that if they crossed the Jordan River he would help them defeat the Canaanites who now occupied the Promised Land. But the people turned away in fear, choosing to continue to live in the desert rather than risk losing to their enemies. If they had trusted God, they would have had some battles, to be sure, but in the end they would have been in a much better position, both physically and spiritually.

The people turned away in fear, choosing to continue to live in the desert.

Despite God's promises and the opportunities that lay before them, they chose "second best." And once the decision was made, there was no turning back. In fact, they tried to change their minds the next day, but God told them it was too late. The die was cast, and their pathway for the next forty years—the rest of their lives, in the case of the adults—was, for the most part, fixed.

We can turn back the hands on our clocks or leave an outdated calendar on the wall, but time marches on nevertheless. Oftentimes the decisions we make are irrevocable. On the honeymoon, we're free to regret our decision to get married, but we can't go back to our wedding day; we can't undo our vows the morning after. There is no use crying, as one teenager did after wrapping his father's car around a tree, "O God, I pray that this accident might not have happened!" Sometimes we get to redo our decisions; most often we don't.

Consequences Multiply

The consequences of Israel's unbelief weren't pretty. They paid an ongoing price for turning away from their God-given opportunity. In fact, they would wander in the wilderness for thirty-eight more years, long enough for all the adults to die in the desert. Only those under the age of twenty at the time of the decision would eventually enter the land—though they would endure the full thirty-eight years in the wilderness as a consequence of their parents' bad decision. This judgment was nonnegotiable. The people had been free to make their decision; they were not free to choose the consequences.

Israel paid an ongoing price for turning away from their God-given opportunity.

We might think it was overkill, but God wanted them to know he does not take gross sin lightly. No wonder there was finger-pointing, anger, and regret among the conflicted multitude. They were bitter and complaining, and especially angry with God, who had led them into the desert in the first place. Moses had to take charge of the unruly nation, and it wasn't easy. In fact, sometime later he became so angry that he struck a rock with his rod rather than speaking to it as God had commanded. For that act of disobedience, he was not allowed to enter the Promised Land.

God wanted them to know he does not take gross sin lightly.

So what did God do now that his people had chosen "second best"? What did he do now that Israel could not undo their decision? The good news is that he did not abandon them. He was not like the father recently on the news who dropped his child off at a city park and never returned. Instead, God took the people by the hand and taught them both the seriousness of disobedience and the wonder of his all-encompassing grace. *He turned their "second best" decision into what became his "first best" future for them.*

We can take courage and find hope in this sad story. God's discipline does not entail his withdrawal from our lives and our circumstances. God will work with us where he finds us—even in the midst of what appears to be an unending wilderness. In the aftermath of our bad decisions, God will do what he always does with his people: He will guide us, provide for us, and forgive us. God does not abandon us when we have made a foolish decision. Sometimes our stupidity unveils his finest moments.

God's discipline does not entail his withdrawal from our lives and our circumstances.

God's Judgment and Grace

"Can God ever bless me again?" That question came to me from a man who had spent two years in prison for his shenanigans as a financial adviser. By deceiving the public by publishing phony reports and hiding his own assets, he had swindled at least a hundred people out of their savings. His closest friends were still angry with him, and his wife and family had walked away when they'd learned of his secret deceit.

He was a Christian, and he said he had never intended to deceive anyone. It all began when he secretly borrowed some money from his firm with the express intention of paying it back. But when he discovered that no one knew what he had done, and when he never quite had the resources to return the funds, he began a cycle of deceit, defrauding the company and his clients in ever-larger amounts.

But when the charade was over, he was left with nothing but his regrets—and the consequences. While sitting in jail where he belonged, he wondered if God could ever bless him again. If he sincerely repented of the crime he had committed, could he still live a productive life, whether behind bars or in freedom? Or does God confine his blessings to good people who don't do such bad things?

I assured him that God has a way of redeeming our lives from the pit—even the pits of our own making. Here are several blessings that God gave to the people of Israel in the desert after they made their wrong turn on the road to the Promised Land. He gave these blessings despite his anger at their unbelief, establishing a pattern of tempering his judgments with grace.

> **God has a way of redeeming our lives from the pit—even the pits of our own making.**

The Blessing of Forgiveness

I'm sure the first question on the minds of the people was, "Can we be forgiven for what we have done?" Moses prayed that God would forgive their disobedience. And God responded by saying, "I have forgiven them, as you asked" (Numbers 14:20). Those words were like a drink of fresh water in the windswept desert. True, the adults would die in the desert, but they would die forgiven. That should breathe hope into the mind of a person who is faced with the stark reality of having sinned and being powerless to undo it. Forgiveness is available.

I have heard some Bible teachers who have given the impression that all the adults who died in the wilderness were unbelievers who forfeited not only the Promised Land but also heaven itself. I don't believe that's true. No doubt some of the people were hardened unbelievers and God judged them for it, but I have no doubt that most of the people deeply repented of their unbelief and their tragic decision, and many—probably the majority—experienced the blessing of God's pardon. Their sin was not beyond God's forgiveness. In Egypt, they had put the blood of the Passover lamb on the doorposts of their houses, which had kept them from God's severe judgment; and now they were forgiven for the great sin of deliberate disobedience.

Still, we should not take the statement about God's pardon as a blanket forgiveness that was given regardless of the attitude of the people's hearts. Having been offered forgiveness, they had to personally receive it. But it was available to those who desired it.

There is hope for the Christian broker who spent time in prison for cheating investors. The woman who has had an abortion must realize that God stands ready to forgive her and to cleanse her troubled conscience. God's grace does not erase the consequences of our sin, but forgiveness does erase the self-incrimination and regret. Forgiveness heals our hearts, even if it doesn't heal our relationships or return the time we have squandered. God always grants forgiveness to those who desire it.* With the past forgiven, there is hope for the future. "If we confess our sins, he is faithful and just and will forgive us our sins and purify us from all unrighteousness" (1 John 1:9).

> **Forgiveness heals our hearts, even if it doesn't heal our relationships or return the time we have squandered.**

The Blessing of Their Children's Inheritance

Although the adult decision makers in Israel's tragic history died in the wilderness, they could take solace in knowing that at least their children would be able to enter the land. What Mom and Dad were not allowed to do, the children would do. "As for your children that you said would be taken as plunder, I will bring them in to enjoy the land you have rejected" (Numbers 14:31). The children suffered for their parents' sins, but not indefinitely. Though their parents had failed them, God had a special blessing for those who were too young to have participated in the decision their parents made.

The young woman who is pregnant, not knowing if she should marry her boyfriend, should not think that she and

---

*The "unpardonable sin" mentioned by Jesus in the New Testament refers to unbelievers who do not desire forgiveness, so it does not apply here.

her child are locked into a life of condemnation because of her sin. I'm sure they will face difficulties, as any single-parent household does, but there can be blessings amid the challenges and regrets.

Children do not have to follow in their parents' footsteps. God's grace is greater than the typical cycle of repeated failure within families. Sometimes the most blessed children come from the most unlikely homes and circumstances. Let's not put up a sign on any home that says, "Grace cannot enter here."

Grace goes where it is most needed and desired. Millions of children with unfaithful—and even evil—parents have served God with faithfulness and great blessing.

A couple named Tony and Ruth exemplify this truth. Tony came from an abusive, alcoholic home, and Ruth was thrown out of her home as a teenager and ended up working on the streets. **God's grace is greater than the typical cycle of repeated failure within families.** Both have been redeemed by God's grace and are raising their children with careful parenting and faith. Together, they are affirming, "The curse stops with us!" And God's grace has thus far proven them right.

The Blessing of Daily Food

God could have simply told the Israelites that it was up to them to find their own food, and let them starve. He could have withdrawn his care, but he didn't. He chose to bless them with manna six days a week, and even added quail meat to their diet when they craved it.

God chose to bless them with manna six days a week. And there is more. "Remember how the LORD your God led you all the way in the wilderness these forty years, to humble and test you in order to know what was in your heart. . . . He humbled you, causing you to hunger and then feeding you with manna. . . . Your clothes did not wear out and your feet did not swell during these forty years" (Deuteronomy 8:2-4). Imagine wearing the same coat for forty years, and even the same sandals. And having food delivered to your doorstep every day.

Food! Clothing! Good health! Not bad care for a group of people who took a wrong turn they could never rectify. God was saying, "Even if you end up someplace you shouldn't, I will not withdraw my love and care." Like the father in the parable of the Prodigal Son (see Luke 15:11-32), God waits for us to turn from our bad decisions, return to him, and restore fellowship. This New Testament promise, "Cast all your anxiety on him because he cares for you" (1 Peter 5:7), isn't just for those who took the right fork in the road; it's also for those who took a wrong turn with deep ruts and washed-out bridges. Even rough paths can be navigated with God's help.

The Blessing of His Guiding Presence

Within the larger community of Israel, there were some who rebelled against Moses' leadership. God took this as a personal affront against his choice of Moses, so he caused the earth to open up and swallow 250 people alive. Later, those who grumbled about what happened also died; in fact, the whole assembly would have died were it not for the intercession of Moses and Aaron.

God waits for us to turn from our bad decisions, return to him, and restore fellowship.

But even in the midst of this harsh discipline, we read, "And behold, the cloud covered it [the tent of meeting] and the glory of the LORD appeared" (Numbers 16:42, NASB). Just imagine, God didn't withdraw; he gave the people another glimpse of his glory. He was there to judge those who had disobeyed him, and he was there to bless those who wanted to worship him. He was there to guide the people as they took their next steps on their monotonous journey. No matter how hot the sand and boring the scenery, God was present to remind them that they were not alone. He'd walk with them as they marked time on their self-chosen path.

Do you want guidance after you have chosen second best? God doesn't promise to guide us if we'd prefer to make our own decisions, but he does lead those who seek him with their whole heart. God's presence is near to all who call upon him, even those who find themselves stranded on the rough patches of a life gone bad.

God didn't withdraw; he gave the people another glimpse of his glory.

We can't walk very far on the wrong road without other forks in the road appearing up ahead. Our options might be limited;

our trail might be lonely and uneventful, but God walks with us. "Do not fear, for I have redeemed you; I have summoned you by name; you are mine. When you pass through the waters, I will be with you; and when you pass through the rivers, they will not sweep over you. When you walk through the fire, you will not be burned" (Isaiah 43:1-2). With God's guidance and companionship, even detours are manageable.

The Blessing of Victory in Battle

Shortly after Moses' brother, Aaron, died in the wilderness, the king of a Canaanite tribe that lived in the Negev Desert captured some Israelites in battle. In response, the Israelites vowed to the Lord, "If you will deliver these people into our hands, we will totally destroy their cities" (Numbers 21:2). We don't understand such a prayer today, but the Israelites in effect were saying, "If you help us destroy the cities of our enemies, we will take nothing for ourselves. Those cities will be an offering to you if you help us achieve victory."

Don't miss this: "The LORD listened to Israel's plea and gave the Canaanites over to them" (Numbers 21:3). We often read that we should listen to the Lord; but here it says that *God* listened to (some translations say *obeyed*) the voices of those who prayed to him. I imagine God was saying, "Yes, you are in the desert being judged for your unbelief, but that does not mean I will stop answering your prayers. I will fight on your behalf; I will still respond to your cries."

You are never in a situation that is beyond God's ability to answer your prayers. Never stop praying; never stop asking; and above all, never stop trusting. Someday you might even give God thanks for the wrong road you have chosen. With that kind of faith, your future is still bright. In fact, with faith in God's sovereignty, we can even thrive after we've chosen "second best."

The Blessing Given to Joshua and Caleb

Are you suffering because of someone else's bad decision? Put yourself in the place of Joshua and Caleb, the two spies who counseled the nation of Israel to believe God. Though they themselves were faithful, they had to wander in the desert for another thirty-eight years, along with everyone else. Remember, when a nation is judged, the righteous suffer along with the disobedient. Still, God honored these men for their faithfulness, even though they inherited the judgment of the desert. And as far as we know, they accepted their plight with dignity and grace.

You are never in a situation that is beyond God's ability to answer your prayers. Never stop praying.

Years later, Joshua became Moses' successor and a famous military commander who not only entered the land but led the nation to multiple victories. Caleb overcame the barriers of peer pressure and race (he was a Kenizzite, not an Israelite) and in his old age entered the Promised Land. When he saw the portion of land he wanted for himself and his descendants, he said to Joshua, the leader of the people, "Give me this hill country that the LORD promised me" (Joshua 14:12). And the Bible tells us, "Then Joshua blessed Caleb . . . and gave him Hebron as his inheritance" (Joshua 14:13). In effect, God responded, "Caleb, because you have followed me whole-heartedly, I will honor you and answer your prayers." At the age of eighty-five, having lived almost half his life in the desert as the result of someone else's sin, Caleb got his request—the fruit of his faith in God. Though we don't like the idea of spending half our lives suffering the consequences of someone else's bad decision, it's encouraging to know that God is still faithful, and he can still redeem our lives and our circum-stances, even if not as quickly as we might like.

You might be a faithful Christian, victimized by the mis-takes and misfortunes of others—your parents, your spouse, a boss, or a friend. You might find yourself tangled up in situa-tions created by others or made worse by others. You need to know that God will not abandon you, even though you may have to experience the repercus-sions of those wrong choices. He sees you, even in the desert others have made for you. As Corrie ten Boom, who survived the horrors of a Nazi concentration camp, put it, "There is no pit so deep that God's love is not deeper still."[1]

God will not abandon you, even in the desert others have made for you.

Our Second Best Can Become God's First Best

The young woman who does not know if she should marry the father of her child—I pray that she makes a wise decision!— might have to walk in the desert of poverty, broken dreams, and the pain of betrayal. But God has not abandoned her to fate. If she accepts God's grace, he will be alongside her, guiding, answering her prayers, and leading her along a new path. Although her "first best" is no longer an option, God can bless her "second best" and even use her predicament for his glory.

The cheater in prison, the woman trapped in a terrible marriage, and the investor who lost money on a get-rich-quick scheme—God does not abandon them if they will turn to him in repentance and faith. Plan A is now forever beyond reach, but plan B can serve God's purposes too. When we foolishly exchange the Promised Land for the desert, God will stay with us in the desert. He has plenty of resources to make our "second best" into a new "first best."

I must emphasize that not everyone in Israel experienced God's forgiveness and grace in the desert. Those who were angry with God and refused to repent perished unforgiven. Grace does not enter closed hearts. Grace must be accepted by those who are willing to submit to God's ways.

When we foolishly exchange the Promised Land for the desert, God will stay with us in the desert.

God can redeem your story, but you must let him, as this poem I came across years ago suggests:

> *As children bring their broken toys,*
> *With tears for us to mend,*
> *I brought my broken dreams to God,*
> *Because He was my friend.*
> *But then instead of leaving Him*

In peace to work alone,
I hung around and tried to help,
With ways that were my own.
At last I snatched them back and cried,
"How can you be so slow?"
"My child" he said, "What could I do?
You never did let go."[2]

In short, grace comes not to the self-assured, but to the desperate. Grace enters when the inner weapons of bitterness, anger, and rebellion are humbly laid at Christ's feet. Jesus said that those who mourn will be comforted (Matthew 5:4) and that the Kingdom of Heaven belongs to the poor in spirit (Matthew 5:3).

God has pulled other people out of the pit ahead of you. You can be next.

A Prayer

Father, forgive me for the wrong turns I have taken on the road of life. I have squandered opportunities; I have disappointed other people and also myself. My whole life appears to be "second best" in comparison to what could have been. Make the best of what I am now giving you. I make this prayer of David my own: "I waited patiently for the LORD; he turned to me and heard my cry. He lifted me out of the slimy pit, out of the mud and mire; he set my feet on a rock and gave me a firm place to stand. He put a new song in my mouth, a hymn of praise to our God. Many will see and fear the LORD and put their trust in him" (Psalm 40:1-3).

3

WHEN YOU'VE MARRIED TROUBLE

You regret that foolish vow

"What a tangled mess!"

That's what I thought to myself when a woman called to tell me her story. She and her boyfriend had said their marriage vows privately so they could be sexually intimate without feeling guilty. A formal marriage was a long way off and they felt they simply could not wait to enjoy sex, so they thought it was better to be married secretly "before God" than to "continue to fornicate," as she put it. To give their secret marriage an aura of respectability, they concocted a very solemn ceremony in a hotel room, with the bride even wearing a wedding dress! God surely would understand, they told themselves; and as for their friends, they didn't need to know.

But as usually happens, a relationship that begins badly ends badly. The man now wanted out of the relationship. He contended they were not legally married, because after all, marriage is more than privately saying vows between the two of you, even if God is brought in as a witness. The woman, on the other hand, took her vows seriously and believed strongly that they were married and he was not free to back out of the deal.

When I spoke to the man to get his side of the story, he said, "Well, yes, certainly we said our vows and all, but I was seduced into marrying her. She carried her wedding dress in the car, knowing I would probably have a weak moment, and I did. I helped her into her wedding dress and then we said our vows and I helped her out of her wedding dress and we made passionate love—although, as you might guess, we had already been intimate before." And then he added, "But this isn't really marriage. You aren't married until it is formalized by a minister and registered with the state. So I'm walking away from what is becoming an ugly relationship."

As usually happens, a relationship that begins badly ends badly.

Well, what do you do when you make a foolish vow? And what happens when you marry trouble? Let's untangle this couple's problem, and then we will discuss how to make the best of a difficult marriage.

The Nature of Vows
For openers, vows differ from promises because all promises have implied conditions. For example, if I were to say, "I'll

meet you at Starbucks for coffee," but then have a car accident en route, you wouldn't call me later and say, "You can't be trusted because you don't keep your promises!" What I actually meant was, "I will meet you at Starbucks if I don't take sick or have an emergency." Conditions were implied.

A vow takes a promise to a higher level and is equivalent to an oath. God takes vows or oaths very seriously. "When you vow a vow to God, do not delay paying it, for he has no pleasure in fools. Pay what you vow. It is better that you should not vow than that you should vow and not pay. Let not your mouth lead you into sin. . . . Why should God be angry at your voice and destroy the work of your hands?" (Ecclesiastes 5:4-6, ESV).

Marriage is the most sacred of all vows or oaths because it has no conditions, implied or otherwise. In committing ourselves to one another "till death do us part," we affirm before God and witnesses that there are no loopholes through which we can wiggle out of our agreement.

The vows stay intact even if the marriage is difficult—which it will almost certainly be. Imagine bringing two self-centered (and even narcissistic) people together in intimacy and expecting them to live in harmony! Add to that the baggage that many bring into their relationships, and it should come as no surprise that the average

A vow takes a promise to a higher level and is equivalent to an oath.

couple faces a huge challenge. And yet it is right here at the point of our weakness and need that God comes to help us.

The couple who said their vows to each other in the hotel room did so voluntarily. They even prayed together and asked God to be a witness to their

It is right here at the point of our weakness and need that God comes to help us.

commitment. In my opinion, they should now follow through with those vows, be committed to each other, and have a public marriage ceremony—for their own benefit. The husband who wants out of the relationship should be man enough to say to his bride, "We made our decision, we confirmed our vows—we are going to resolve our differences and make this marriage work!" God gives special blessing to the one who fears the Lord and "keeps an oath even when it hurts, and does not change" (Psalm 15:4).

Of course, there was nothing the wife could do to make her husband fulfill his vow. As it turned out, the more she tried to convince him to stay, the more determined he was to leave. People walk away from their vows all the time, as evidenced by the millions of divorces annually in our society. We can walk away from a vow, but we cannot walk away from God, who holds us accountable for what we have promised.

If anyone would suggest that I'm giving teenagers permission to "get married" by saying their vows privately so they can have sex without guilt, please understand that I am saying just the opposite. Like the couple I mentioned, anyone who gets married secretly so they can legitimatize sex can expect nothing but guilt, incrimination, and anger directed against one another. Whenever sex is more important than integrity; when the permanent is willingly sacrificed on the altar of the immediate; when one person uses another (or for that matter, each uses the other), the end result is always pain, regret, anger, and emotional baggage. "I was married by a judge," said a friend of mine. "Now I wish I had asked for a jury!"

The Day God Blessed a Foolish Vow

Can God bless a foolish vow? Of course. His blessing won't change a foolish vow into a wise one, but he can and does make the best of our foolish decisions, often showing his power and grace when it is most needed. There is a story in the Old Testament that confirms this.

After Israel moved into the Promised Land, God explicitly told Joshua not to make a covenant with any of the tribes within the borders of Canaan (Deuteronomy 7:1-2). But one day a caravan of nomads came to Joshua, claiming they had come from beyond the borders of the land. They begged him to make a peace treaty with them because they feared they would otherwise be destroyed. Incredibly, though Joshua was a man who consistently obeyed God, in this instance he "did not ask counsel from the LORD" (Joshua 9:14, ESV). So without consulting God, but simply believing the Gibeonites' story, Joshua vowed to protect them. Only days later, he discovered that he had been fooled.

We cannot walk away from God, who holds us accountable for what we have promised.

On a purely human level, Joshua might have been tempted to back out of his vow because, as it turned out,

Joshua chose to live with the consequences of his foolish vow.

these strangers did not come from beyond the borders of Israel; they lived just across the valley. A lesser man might have said, "I am going to break my vow because they lied about who they were." Not Joshua. He chose to live with the consequences of his foolish vow. He had sworn to them by the Lord God of Israel, and now he would not touch them, as promised.

God was not confused by all this. As we might expect, he chose to make the best of Joshua's bad decision. To the benefit of Israel, these pagans were allowed to live with the Israelites as servants. Although they were a thorn in Israel's side, they performed important chores, such as cutting wood and carrying water. Though the Gibeonites were condemned to perpetual service, centuries later the record shows that they were still working in the Temple area, honored by serving the living God (Joshua 9:27; Nehemiah 7:6-7, 25).

And it gets even better. Because Joshua kept his vow, Israel saw a rare display of God's power. After news spread that the Gibeonites had made a treaty with Joshua, a coalition of kings decided to attack them, since they were now in league with Joshua. So Joshua—because of his vow—had to defend the Gibeonites in the ensuing battle. In the process, he witnessed one of the greatest miracles in the entire Bible—both the sun and the moon standing still in the heavens until Joshua won the battle. The divine commentary reads, "There has been no day like it before or since, when the LORD obeyed the voice of a man, for the LORD fought for Israel" (Joshua 10:14, ESV).

What an understatement! We would never have had this marvelous story if Joshua had broken his vow. Yes, God obeyed the voice of Joshua and said in effect, "Although the vow you made was presumptuous, I will use your circumstances to show you one of the greatest miracles I have ever performed on planet Earth!"

Here is a promise to keep before us. King David asked in Psalm 15:1, "LORD, who may dwell in your sacred tent? Who may live on your holy mountain?" He answers the question by listing those who qualify for such special blessings; among them is the man who keeps an oath "even when it hurts" (15:4).

For those who have married unwisely, and for all who make promises that are difficult to keep, you can still expect to receive God's blessing. Spiritual blessings await those who don't back out of a vow just because their situation has changed.

Spiritual blessings await those who don't back out of a vow just because their situation has changed.

One wife wrote a letter to me telling of how horrible she felt on her wedding day. She married her boyfriend only because he had pushed her toward intimacy, and once having crossed that line, she felt an obligation to go through with the wedding. Her parents, knowing nothing about her anguish, encouraged her to marry the man. If she could have run away somewhere on her wedding day, she would have; she not only didn't love him, she knew that this was a disaster in the making.

Two things held their marriage together in those early days. First, divorce was not an option. They took their vows seriously and did not think it was right to walk away from a difficult situation. Second, even though they were, at best, nominal Christians when they married, they chose to become involved in a church; they connected with other couples and refused to struggle alone. They also had the added blessing of their parents' prayers. For years, they struggled, but today they are in mission work. They are proof that sometimes marriages that begin badly can end well, through much prayer and agony.

God can turn a curse into a blessing even in a difficult marriage. Don't look for an escape hatch when the going becomes difficult.

Before You Divorce

"Marriage," someone has said, "is like having open-heart surgery without anesthesia." Heartbreaking stories are everywhere: A man wrote to tell me that his wife, who spent hours on the Internet, had hooked up through Facebook with a lover she'd known during college. A woman told me she discovered that her husband had cheated on her and now didn't know if she should divorce him. Another woman said her husband had gambled away their savings without her knowing it.

> **God can turn a curse into a blessing even in a difficult marriage. Don't look for an escape hatch.**

Divorce seems so attractive in such instances, but it is usually not the great deliverance many people expect it to be. That decision most often leads to endless entanglements, vengeance, anger, and regret. Worse, if children are involved, they often suffer and take their pain into the next generation.

Divorce seems so attractive, but it is usually not the great deliverance many people expect it to be.

Lou Priolo, a divorce counselor of many years, writes, "Most [who divorce] have come back in one way or another and acknowledged that the suffering they experienced was much greater than they initially thought it would be. . . . They invariably told me that if they had it to do over again, they wouldn't."[1]

Somewhere I read that there are two things that should not be done prematurely: embalming and divorce. Of course, I'm not saying that a marriage partner should put up with persistent physical, emotional, or verbal abuse, either. This is especially true if there are children in the home who can be damaged by an abusive parent. I suggest that the suffering partner go for help quickly and that the offending partner be warned that he or she will be exposed.

Many marriages are unhappy for one reason or another. The relationship is not abusive per se, but strained or emotionally dead. Such marriages must be rescued. Furthermore, help must be given to those who wish to divorce for any number of reasons, including the oft-given rationale that "I've found my soul mate."

I've observed five myths that people are prone to believe when they want out of their marriage. These myths, which almost always lead to divorce, are devastating to marriages and families.

1. *My happiness is what is most important.* "I can't believe that God would want me to be unhappy for the rest of my life," a man told me. "Christianity teaches fulfillment and happiness, and I know that this marriage is a real burden, not a blessing. I can't take it, and if I divorce, my kids will adjust."

Let me say clearly that faithfulness is much more important than happiness!

Imagine Jesus in Gethsemane, saying, "I'm not going to the cross, because it interferes with my happiness." He might have avoided the pain of hard obedience, but the world would have been unredeemed. Even more ominously, his Father in heaven would not have been pleased. Obedience, not happiness, should be our first priority.

A man who left his wife after thirty years to marry his dream girl dropped dead three months after the wedding. If he had known that he was going to give an account to God so soon, he might have stayed in his first marriage, whether it was fulfilling or not. The simple fact is that we don't know the future; we don't know what speed bumps will cross our paths when we think that our happiness is more important than our faithfulness.

Faithfulness is much more important than happiness!

Peter Marshall, the famous past chaplain of the US Senate,

once said, "Once and for all, we must put out of our minds that the purpose of life here is to enjoy ourselves. . . . That is not what life is about. You were put here for a purpose, and that purpose is not related to superficial pleasures. You do not have a right to happiness; you have the right to nothing."[2]

We have no right to happiness, but we do have the obligation of obedience to God. But when we put obedience above our own happiness, we find that we are blessed. Ultimately, there is no conflict between what God requires and what is best for us.

There is no conflict between what God requires and what is best for us.

Discipleship means that we make tough decisions in favor of others rather than ourselves, and especially that we live with an eye toward pleasing God. If we are faithful, all suffering—including marital suffering—will eventually result in our ultimate benefit and God's glory.

2. *Finding the right person will give me real fulfillment.* I'm sure you've heard some variation of the following rationalization: "Finally, I've found my soul mate. It's as if there was a piece of a puzzle that was missing, and now I've found it. It's not sexual. We can just talk for hours, and somehow she (or he) is tapping something deep within me that I never even knew existed." Next comes a separation, because the wayward partner wants time to "think things through." The divorce almost inevitably follows.

When we look at the moon from Earth, we always see only one side; but there is a back side of the moon—the dark side—that we never see. In the very same way, couples go into marriage not realizing that their partner has a dark side. Soon after the wedding, that dawning reality might bring immediate, crushing disappointment; but as couples work through their pain, they can emerge with confidence, strength, and maturity in their relationship. In the process, they learn the meaning of sacrificial love.

This scenario has played itself out a thousand times: A woman whose husband mostly ignores her meets a man who just adores her; he enjoys her accent and takes note of many details about her. She says, "Finally, I have found the man of my dreams." But after she divorces and remarries, she discovers that the euphoria wears off quickly and she wakes up to the knowledge that her new man is self-centered, controlling, and manipulative. Although almost half of all first marriages end in divorce, more than 60 percent of all second marriages end in divorce. Unresolved conflicts from the first marriage are carried into the second marriage; and having divorced once, the second time is easier.

> **As couples work through their pain, they can emerge with confidence, strength, and maturity in their relationship.**

Thirty years ago, one of our deacons at Moody Church told me, "I'm leaving my wife because I am in a dry desert and now I've found an oasis." Ten years later, he wrote me a ten-page letter, a tale of woe and grief. He explained how his marvelous "oasis" turned out to be as bitter as gall. His new wife eventually rejected him and threw him out of the house.

If I remember correctly, one of their children committed suicide. This ex-deacon confessed that the dry desert would have been better than the stagnant, poisoned marsh in which he now found himself. It does not take long for a beautiful dream to end in a nightmare.

It is much better to *be* the right person than to *find* the right person. Every one of us has flaws and weaknesses; we have perverse thoughts and desires that crave fulfillment. Even the most compatible person you meet might turn out to be angry, vengeful, and unfaithful in a marriage. And if you didn't find the right person the first time, you will likely not find the right person the second time.

It is much better to *be* the right person than to *find* the right person.

3. *I can still be a caring person, even if I break up our marriage to marry my dream partner.* Just this week, a man confided in me that his brother had said to him, "I'm having an affair; but whatever you do, don't tell my wife, because I just love her and my children." We can talk ourselves into endless lies; we want to believe these lies so badly that we are willing to overlook the obvious fact that if we cared more about others than ourselves, we would never fool ourselves into thinking that selfishly leaving a marriage is consistent with *love*. Still, we believe these lies in broad daylight.

Even an emotional affair with another woman kills a man's romantic feelings toward his wife and consumes the psychic energy needed for being an involved father to his children. A man who tells himself that he can still love his wife and children while he selfishly has his mind focused on another woman has talked himself into lies he is anxious to believe. Almost always,

Even an emotional affair with another woman kills a man's romantic feelings toward his wife.

a partner cannot get out of a marriage relationship without deliberate self-deception. No, you don't love your wife and children if you are willing to leave them to find the partner of your dreams.

4. *I can manage the consequences. God will forgive me, then I can move on.* Many years ago, a pastor who had left his wife for another woman said to me, "Oh, sure, I'm sinning, but remember, even David got his Bathsheba." Yes, that's true. David did get his Bathsheba; and along with her, he got endless grief for his family and disaster for his entire kingdom. Yes, God forgave David, because God is gracious, but the disastrous consequences went on—not just here on earth, but also into eternity. David's family was destroyed and his sons died without a hint of repentance.

To have the attitude "I haven't done anything that a little forgiveness can't solve" is to seriously insult God. There are certain built-in consequences of divorce that are not removed when we repent; hidden dominoes that, when they fall, reverberate throughout our families and our spheres of influence. And the damage done to ourselves, our mates, our children, and more generally to the people of God is beyond calculation. Just as it is impossible to plant poison ivy and reap tomatoes, so it is impossible to have an unbiblical divorce and expect a good outcome.

5. *He/she will never change.* Somewhere I read that many couples are like windshield wipers that never meet. Each partner does his or her "dance," but they are never really on the same page. They argue about the same things year after year after year. Nothing is ever resolved. So they learn to survive under the same roof, but the rule is, "I stay in my sphere and you stay in yours; I push your buttons when I'm angry and you push mine." But like those windshield wipers, they just keep going on and on and on without connecting.

There are certain built-in consequences of divorce that are not removed when we repent.

We must never give up hope, even in the worst of marriages. My wife, Rebecca, and I are close friends with a couple who intended to divorce for several reasons, including the husband's seeming inability to stop flirting with other women and his penchant for making unwise financial decisions. Of course, as in many marriages, anger on both sides had erupted over any number of other issues. Before the divorce papers were signed, however, the husband came to realize the foolishness of his behavior; he realized that he and his wife had so much going for them, if only they could step back and see their relationship objectively. Most important, both parties were led to repentance before

We must never give up hope, even in the worst of marriages.

God and became painfully honest in their communication, something they had not experienced in years. Today they are an example of a happily married couple whose relationship was rescued from the brink of disaster.

There are thousands of living examples of couples who have stayed together, worked through their differences, and are happily reconciled. Many couples have recovered from infidelity, addictions, and even "irreconcilable differences." What if God wants to show his power by changing you and your mate?

Of course, there might be times when divorce, tragically, is the only option, especially when there is repeated immorality or persistent abuse. But most people who divorce regret it for years to come, and many spend the rest of their lives picking up the pieces.

Making the Best of a Bad Marriage

How can you make the best of a bad marriage? Or more accurately, how does God make the best of your bad marriage? He does not abandon you at the point of your need. When he doesn't change your partner, he changes you. A bad or challenging marriage is a laboratory in which God's faithfulness can be seen most clearly against the backdrop of human failure and regret. You must invite God to walk with you through the difficult valleys and deep tunnels of your marriage. His faithfulness is seen not just when the sun is shining, but also when darkness envelops your closest relationship. The greater your need, the greater God's available grace.

> **A challenging marriage is a laboratory in which God's faithfulness can be seen most clearly.**

How should we respond to an unhappy relationship?

Here's the basic rule: *When sinned against, do not sin in return.* Too often, marital strife is made worse by retaliation, cursing, threats, and vengeance. The New Testament clearly teaches that we should avoid such responses. Jesus himself did not retaliate, but "he entrusted himself to him who judges justly" (1 Peter 2:23). He was willing to wait for God to bring justice to his situation. Difficult marriages are training grounds for developing the fruit of a godly character.

Here are some steps we can take to make the best of a bad situation.

Keep God at the Center

Most Christian couples, I would imagine, pray about their marriage problems, and they can be disappointed when God doesn't seem to answer. Quite frankly, one reason that God may seem silent is that, although they may have prayed, they haven't committed their marriage and their future wholly to him. In fact, "praying together" can be a substitute for genuine obedience. To say, "I'm praying about it" gives their actions a degree of respectability, when actually they have given up on the marriage and are refusing the grace that God extends to them to persevere with a difficult partner.

To commit yourself and your marriage to God means much more than praying about it; rather it involves surrendering yourself, your mate, and your future to God, subject to his will and purpose. I've counseled couples who have resisted this step for fear that God will ask them to do something they detest—such as stay in the marriage, for example. What they don't realize is that as we go through the process of submitting our lives fully to God, he grants the strength we need to follow through with obedience. In other words, God supplies the strength to do what he commands us to do. In the midst of our trials, he gives us a way of escape—not from the marriage, but from the snares that would tempt us to give up on the marriage—so that we can endure (1 Corinthians 10:13).

God supplies the strength to do what he commands us to do.

In our culture, we're obsessed with defining ourselves by our woundedness. Many people who were abused or betrayed years ago keep their emotional wounds as open sores. They have a ready excuse for their anger, their desire to control, and their self-justifying responses; it's as if the abuse of the past is still happening. Having been sinned against, they act as if they now have license to sin against others. Their heightened sense of justice fuels their continuing anger; to surrender and release their resentment to God would be to minimize the offense against them.

But here is a liberating truth: God's grace extends to all who are willing to surrender their desire for justice to him. When he says, "It is mine to avenge; I will repay" (Deuteronomy 32:35), he removes from our shoulders the burden of getting even. Surrendering our wounds to God is difficult but not impossible. Through our willingness to refuse retaliation and extend forgiveness, we receive "grace upon grace" (John 1:16, NASB). The open wound becomes a scar, because healing is taking place—and will continue.

Examine Yourself

Here is a bit of wisdom that will help you through many difficulties: When something goes wrong in your marriage, rather than think that your spouse is at fault, try taking responsibility yourself. Your first thought should be, "I am at fault!" One partner usually bears greater responsibility for the failure of the marriage, but seldom is one partner wholly responsible. A root cause in marital strife is that we seldom want to "own our own stuff," as the saying goes. As someone has said, "The ability to see ourselves as our partner sees us is a divine gift."

> **God's grace extends to all who are willing to surrender their desire for justice to him.**

Search your own soul to grasp your part in the conflict. I've known so many people who have complained to me about their mate while hauling around their own huge, unacknowledged baggage. Put a pencil in a glass of water and it will appear crooked. Likewise, our perception of others, and our perception of ourselves, is always skewed. To see ourselves for what we truly are is so painful that many of us build elaborate defenses for our own insecurities and shortcomings. Anger, pride, and selfishness cause us to see everyone else (particularly our marriage partners) as "bent."

Sometimes, in counseling, I'll ask each partner to list

the other's faults. The response is usually swift; most of the time, they ask for more writing paper! Then I ask them to list their own weaknesses, to acknowledge their own failures and sins. Now there are long pauses, and they roll their eyes as if they have nothing to write down. Soon it becomes clear that they see their spouse's faults with 20/20 vision, but are blind to their own. Often through years of rationalization, some partners have insulated themselves from seeing themselves as they truly are.

Our perception of others, and our perception of ourselves, is always skewed.

People are sometimes unconscious of their own anger, laziness, controlling personality, wastefulness, or obsessions. Some hold their mate to impossible standards and yet are unpredictable in their own responses. Some are defensive, never able to admit to being wrong. All the while they do not face up to the deep unresolved needs that prevent them from giving and receiving love. A wife may seek to control her husband through manipulation, bad moods, and threats. She may deliberately set up barriers in their relationship so that when he becomes angry, she can blame their dispute on him. If she harbors unresolved resentments, she may not be able to receive her husband's love and may subconsciously make it impossible for him to love her. If she fears intimacy, she will make sure

Some people see their spouse's faults with 20/20 vision, but are blind to their own.

that her marriage is in a constant state of conflict so that she can deny sex to her husband.

The husband, on the other hand, may become passive-aggressive, deliberately not communicating—and when he does, limiting his comments to *yes* or *no*, or even worse, a grunt. He wants to make sure his wife and family know that he is angry, and in his mind he is more than justified in refusing to give of himself to their needs and concerns. He may also set up barriers to the relationship, believing it's his wife's responsibility to change her ways or ask forgiveness. Refusing to communicate and cooperate puts everyone on notice: "I've been wronged; I'm angry and I have a right to be, considering the way I am treated." The idea that he might be responsible, or at least partially responsible, for the breakdown of the marriage never enters his mind.

Some partners have lived with denial for so long that they cannot benefit from spiritual counsel. All correction is dismissed with hostile rationalizations. Sometimes only a traumatic event will awaken them so that they can see themselves with a degree of objectivity. They are defensive because they fear exposure of their own hollowness and insecurity.

Counselors can help, but they can only go so far. God must break into our souls so that we are able to see ourselves as God sees us apart from Christ. Marital harmony can only begin when we pray with David, "Search me, O God, and know my heart; try me and know my anxious thoughts; and see if there be any hurtful way in me, and lead me in the everlasting way" (Psalm 139:23-24, NASB).

Learn the Lesson of Forgiveness

"Whatever you don't forgive, you pass on!" This bit of wisdom is crucial if we are going to avoid inflicting our sins on the next generation. Without forgiveness, there is no hope of peace and tranquility in our relationships.

Because a later chapter focuses on the topic of how to resolve disputes with people whom we have wronged, we will focus here on the single question of how to forgive our mate when he or she has wronged us. People often come to marriage with deep insecurities or unacknowledged abandonment issues. To make matters worse, they may also be unaware of how their past affects their mate. When they marry, in effect they are saying, "Partner, heal my wound, but please don't touch it or I will become angry, resentful, judgmental, and impossible to live with." Unfortunately, to heal a wound without touching it is like trying to fill the Grand Canyon with a shovel.

Some partners have lived with denial for so long that they cannot benefit from spiritual counsel.

How do we live with an attitude of forgiveness? How do we not become bitter when constantly wronged? We must be secure in the knowledge that we ourselves have been forgiven and are loved by God. Only this can give us a forgiving spirit. We need God's help to act on what we know to be true: Forgiveness is a choice that can be made whether we feel like it or not.

For true reconciliation to take place, three things must happen: (1) forgiveness must be both requested and granted; (2) trust must be restored; and (3) respect must dominate the relationship. But the true test is that once we have forgiven and been reconciled, the past can no longer control the future relationship. A man told me that years ago he had confessed to an affair and his wife had said she forgave him; but whenever they got into an argument, the affair became her trump card, and "she would bring it up and wipe my nose in the dirt."

Forgiveness is a choice that can be made whether we feel like it or not.

God doesn't treat us that way. When we confess our sins, he forgives us. We are left with the consequences but not the guilt or the tortured conscience. Someone said about a married couple after an argument, "They buried the hatchet, but the grave was shallow and well marked." And a trail to the site was no doubt visible.

What if our mate wrongs us and does not ask for forgiveness? We must seek help for the relationship, but meanwhile we must live faithfully, just as God remains faithful to us despite the unacknowledged sin in our lives. We cannot change our mate's heart or behavior, but God can—and sometimes he does

Once we have forgiven and been reconciled, the past can no longer control the future.

when we ask him to change *our* hearts first. Without minimizing the depth of the pain caused by those who refuse to own up to their faults, we might have to live with unresolved issues. Read this poignant observation by Reinhold Niebuhr:

> Forgiving love is a possibility only for those who know that they are not good, who feel themselves in need of divine mercy, who live in a dimension deeper and higher than that of moral idealism, feel themselves as well as their fellow men convicted of sin by a holy God and know that the differences between the good man and the bad man are insignificant in his sight.[3]

Forgiveness—especially when unrequested by the person in need of it—is difficult and requires extra grace. Such forgiveness in itself does not bring true reconciliation, but it does bring a measure of peace to a troubled marriage. By God's grace, it can become a bridge to eventually bring husband and wife together.

When a marriage goes bad, our first question should not be, How do I get out of this to avoid further pain? It should rather be, How can I bring glory to God through this painful experience? God can help us avoid marital storms, but sometimes he just walks through them with us. In the process, we develop endurance, patience, and faith.

The Rewards of Endurance

James Fraser, an eighteenth-century Scottish pastor, was known to have a very obstinate wife. When he returned home in the evening, he went directly to his study, avoiding the room where his wife was, or else he would receive a tongue-lashing. His wife controlled the lamp oil and the coal, and she would not allow him a fire to warm him in his room. During the winter, because he was so cold, he walked back and forth in his dark study with his hands extended in front of him. After he died, they found indentations in the plaster where his hands had hit the wall during his nightly routine.

When other pastors praised their wives, he chimed in, "My wife has been better to me than all of yours put together. . . . She has driven me to my knees seven times a day, and that is more than any of your wives have done for you!"

Fraser made the best of a difficult marriage. He realized that every difficulty has its benefits if we respond to it correctly. He knew that problems have a purifying effect and that suffering in marriage is part of the refining process.

Forgiveness does not bring true reconciliation, but it does bring a measure of peace to a troubled marriage.

When married to trouble, claim this promise: "Sacrifice thank offerings to God, fulfill your vows to the Most High, and call on me in the day of trouble; I will deliver you, and you will honor me" (Psalm 50:14-15).

A Prayer

Father, today I give you my marriage; I transfer to your capable hands all of the burdens that have come with my vows. Help me to realize that I cannot change my mate, but *you* can. I turn my spouse over to you, believing you are able to do what I cannot. Help me to stop criticizing, manipulating, and judging my partner, but to show love and tolerance. Turn our regrets into blessings and our painful past into reasons to give you praise.

4

WHEN YOU'VE CROSSED A MORAL BOUNDARY

Your secret is exposed

David is the last man you'd expect to find in such a mess. He committed adultery with another man's wife and then murdered her husband to cover up the deed. Though he made his selfish decision in the privacy of his own home, his bad judgment had far-reaching personal and public consequences. He caused a woman, whose proper allegiance was to her husband, to compromise, and they both would have to cope with an unwanted pregnancy. He forfeited his moral authority in the lives of his children and then lived to see his family and kingdom come unraveled. And yet despite the horrific consequences of David's sin, God found a way to make the best of David's disastrous decision.

This chapter is written for a friend of mine whose fifteen-year-old granddaughter just had a baby with a young man scarcely older than she. It is written for everyone who has discovered—much to their chagrin—that even one illicit sexual liaison can boomerang with countless unexpected consequences. And it is written for everyone who has committed a sexual sin and now wonders whether God can forgive them and bring some redemption out of their predicament.

Even one illicit sexual liaison can boomerang with countless unexpected consequences.

Every human being is a sexual creature. It's impossible to estimate the amount of energy and effort expended every day by people fantasizing about sexuality. We live in a sex-saturated culture that ridicules chastity before marriage as a vestige of a repressed era best left behind. Even the idea of a one-man-with-one-woman committed relationship is thought too restrictive. Millions find out too late that there are good reasons for saving one's virginity till marriage and for being faithful to one partner "till death do us part." But today, many people tell themselves that sex outside of marriage can't be wrong, because their relationship is so fulfilling or beautiful—or they have met their "soul mate." We are all tempted to believe such lies because our desires are so powerful and unrelenting. The human mind has the capacity to rationalize anything the heart really wants.

King David was approximately forty-seven years old when he embarked on a path that would haunt him for the rest of his life. In fact, I think it would have been better if he had died a year before this story unfolded. Our memory of him as a leader, as a king, as a "man after God's own heart" would not have to include the dark blot that skews his otherwise outstanding legacy. And yet, there is one great reason we can be thankful for David's failure: We see what God can do to make the best of a very bad decision.

You know the story, as recorded in 2 Samuel 11. David stayed home from the battlefield when he should have been out leading his army. One day he awakened from a rooftop nap and glanced across the way to where a beautiful woman was taking an afternoon bath. David's blood ran hot and he immediately schemed to get the woman for himself. In the heat of his passion, he set aside concern for his integrity, his moral authority, and his family—not to mention Bathsheba and her fam-

The human mind has the capacity to rationalize anything the heart really wants.

ily. His concentration on the one thing he desired at that moment blocked everything else out of his mind.

The Steps Leading to Moral Failure

David's downward spiral is consistent with a familiar pattern followed by many who have fallen into sexual sin.

First, he *saw* a woman.

"It happened, late one afternoon, when David arose from his couch and was walking on the roof of the king's house, that he saw from the roof a woman bathing; and the woman was very beautiful" (2 Samuel 11:2, ESV). His sexual desires were quickly awakened as he gazed at her beautiful form.

His concentration on the one thing he desired at that moment blocked everything else out of his mind.

He looked, and then he stared; he observed, and then he obsessed. He created in his own mind a scenario that he would soon enact.

We should pause long enough to ponder what David did *not* see. He didn't see the shame that would eventually come to him; he didn't foresee that his four sons would eventually be destroyed because of his scheme. He didn't foresee the disintegration of his kingdom. How different it might have been if David had been able to foresee the hidden consequences that would eventually erupt and destroy everything that was important to him. But for now, all that really mattered was the euphoria of the present moment. He didn't consciously rebel against God when he planned to connect with Bathsheba; he simply ignored God for a moment.

David wasn't thinking, "I hate God and his commandments!" At such moments, our minds are not filled with hatred for God, just forgetfulness of God. Like one man embarking on a similar path told me, "I am going to enjoy myself today and then deal with the devil and God tomorrow." The present enticing moment tempts us to suspend all rational judgment. We *feel* instead of *think*.

Imagine what a different ending there would have been to this story if David had prayed, "God, I want to thank you for creating such a beautiful woman. I know that she belongs to another man. And God, I also want to thank you for all the wonderful wives you have given me; thank you for my children and the many blessings toward me that are undeserved. You have been so good to me; please let me be satisfied with what you have already given me." And with that, he should have turned around and gone into his house.

At such moments, our minds are not filled with hatred for God, just forgetfulness of God.

Instead, David pulled anchor and embarked on a river whose current and depth were increasing. Around the bend were ferocious rapids, but he couldn't see them from where his perilous journey began. Soon the speed and momentum of his boat would be beyond his control. There would be no stopping now that he had listened to his feelings instead of his mind.

It all began when David *saw*.

Then David *sent*.

"And David sent and inquired about the woman" (2 Samuel 11:3, ESV). Wouldn't you like to know what he said to his servants when he sent them to "inquire"? Maybe it was something like this: "You know, I've been living in this neighborhood for a long time. It just dawned on me that I don't know

There would be no stopping now that he had listened to his feelings instead of his mind.

our neighbors very well. I wonder if you'd find out who lives in that house over there, because someday we may want to throw a block party, and we have to know who we're going to invite."

No doubt David lied about his intentions. A person who commits sexual sin has already made up his mind to lie— and why not? When you've decided to betray your spouse in immorality, a lie seems trivial in comparison. Once you've broken one of the commandments, breaking another one seems easy, and possibly even *right*. Hiding our sin entails deceit, and deceit entails lying.

David *saw*.

David *sent*.

David *took*.

"So David sent messengers and took her, and she came to him, and he lay with her" (2 Samuel 11:4, ESV). We want to know if Bathsheba gave in to the king's advances because of the prestige of being attractive to royalty, or whether she did so out of a sense of duty; no doubt her expectation was that whatever the king wanted, the king got. Or perhaps she said, "At last I've found my soul mate; my husband Uriah spends a good deal of time in the army, so we've grown apart."

When you've decided to betray your spouse in immorality, a lie seems trivial in comparison. We can imagine that David's heart and mind were in conflict. We can surmise he felt both the euphoria of sexual attraction and the apprehension of knowing he was about to do something he would not have tolerated from anyone who served him. After sleeping with Bathsheba, David probably thought it was a one-night stand. She could return to her house and all would be well. If there were suspicions, it would be the word of the king against hers.

But illicit relationships are never as compartmentalized as we hope they will be. Somehow, sexual sin always has unintended consequences, and the effects spill over into other relationships and areas of life. Like Eve, who saw only the fruit of the forbidden tree and not its poisonous effects, David and Bathsheba probably thought that after their rendezvous their relationship would end as quickly as it began. But it didn't. And it never does.

Illicit relationships are never as compartmentalized as we hope they will be.

Let's suppose that Bathsheba had not become pregnant. Would she and David have been able to "get by" with their secret encounter? They might have avoided the need to cover their sin, but by no means would their lives have returned to normal without other consequences.

First of all, they would have to live with their own guilt; they would have feelings that could not simply be ignored or unlearned. What is more, there would be fear—the suspicion that others already knew what had happened.

Second, both would have to keep their secret from their spouses. This might have been easier for David, who had many wives, than for Bathsheba, who had only one husband. When Uriah returned from the battle, she would've had to resort to deceit, pretending she'd been chaste in his absence.

Not only that, but David and Bathsheba would likely have

continued their secret liaison. Having once experienced the oneness that comes through sexual intercourse, they would have had powerful reasons to maintain the connection in order to recreate the euphoria of their first night together. Once you've overstepped the boundaries, it is easy to do so again.

But now Bathsheba was pregnant, a matter that needed to be addressed. If it had happened in our day, she might have had a secret abortion. But that was not an option. So now there was a third person involved in the relationship. This baby would change everything. When Bathsheba communicated the news of her pregnancy to David, he knew that they had a predicament that needed a solution.

The Cover-Up

When our sin threatens to be exposed, we often resort to elaborate cover-ups in an effort to keep our wrongdoing concealed and the consequences at bay. David was no different—though we have no evidence that Bathsheba was even aware of David's plan.

Plan A was to bring Uriah back from the battlefield to sleep with his wife. It seemed like a foolproof plan. After weeks or months of deprivation, what husband wouldn't want to "catch up" with his wife? If Uriah slept with Bathsheba and she was later found to be pregnant, no one would be the wiser. David even gave Uriah some gifts, evidently hoping to spark romance with his beautiful wife.

When our sin threatens to be exposed, we often resort to elaborate cover-ups.

But Uriah was such a good soldier that he refused to enjoy the comforts of home while his fellow soldiers were camping in the field. Instead, he slept outside the king's palace and did not even go home to see his wife.

So plan A failed.

David then schemed to get Uriah drunk, thinking that this might make him forget his loyalty to his fellow soldiers. But as someone once observed, Uriah was a better man drunk than David was sober. He again refused to go home to his wife and again slept outside the palace.

Let's pause to consider: What should David have done right from the beginning when he faced his predicament? He should have called Uriah home and confessed, "Uriah, your wife is pregnant and I'm the father of the child," and then they could have discussed issues of custody and the like. Admittedly, that would have been a difficult conversation, but it would have been better than the scenario that unfolded. David opted for what initially *appeared* to be an easier path; but if he had confessed his sin and taken his strong medicine right from the get-go, he would not have had to deal with the greater sorrows that his cover-up would bring.

What should David have done right from the beginning when he faced his predicament?

Think for a moment about what would have happened if former president Bill Clinton had admitted to his affair with Monica Lewinsky immediately, rather than lying about it under oath and prolonging both the investigation and his own shame. Truth—even embarrassing truth—always serves us better than deceit.

When plan A and plan B both fell through, David reasoned that there are times when a man has to do what a man has to do. Whenever we start down the road of deceit and deception, trying to cover up our sin, the stakes inevitably escalate. There are times when career and reputation seem much more important than integrity. In David's case, with the power and authority of the kingdom at his disposal, the escalation soon got out of hand. He sent Uriah back to the battlefield with a letter to his commander, Joab, that said, "Put Uriah out in front where the fighting is fiercest. Then withdraw from him so he will be struck down and die" (2 Samuel 11:15).

When a messenger came to the palace to report Uriah's death, David said to him, "Say this to Joab: 'Don't let this upset you; the sword devours one as well as another. Press the attack against the city and destroy it.' Say this to encourage Joab" (2 Samuel 11:25). In effect, David was saying, "Life is tough. You win some, you lose some. Don't let the death of a soldier trouble you, because it's not going to trouble me." Another consequence of covered-up sin is that it tends to sear the conscience, hardening our hearts to what is good and true and noble. How else could David respond with such callousness?

> **Whenever we start down the road of deceit and deception, the stakes inevitably escalate.**

At this point, let us pause for a moment and ask, How well is the cover-up working? David knows the truth, Bathsheba knows the truth, Joab knows the truth—and the people of Jerusalem are soon going to know the truth (they can count to nine months). Moreover, the prophet Nathan is about to learn the truth, because, more

Covered-up sin tends to sear the conscience, hardening our hearts to what is good and true and noble.

ominously, *God* knows the truth. Notice how the chapter ends: "But the thing David had done displeased the LORD" (2 Samuel 11:27).

David pretended that the cover-up was working; and if it wasn't working, he didn't want to know about it. He learned to suppress his troubled conscience for the sake of his personal reputation and the supposed good of his country.

Sometimes you just want to stifle that pesky internal voice.

But God, who loved David too much to let him get by with this, sent a prophet to jerk him back into reality. And God loves you too much to let you get by with such sins.

David's Heart Revealed

The prophet Nathan used a simple story—with a powerful point—to get David's attention (see 2 Samuel 12). In the story, a traveler comes to visit a rich man who has many flocks and herds; but rather than slaughter one of his own lambs to feed his guest, the rich man takes the one little ewe lamb belonging to his poor neighbor.

When David heard what had happened, he became white-hot with anger and said, "The man who did this must die! He must pay for that lamb four times over, because he did such a thing and had no pity" (2 Samuel 12:5-6).

David was so intent on self-justification that he magnified someone else's sin and minimized his own.

Unknowingly, he had just sprung his own trap. Nathan responded with a verbal arrow to the king's heart: "*You* are the man!" (2 Samuel 12:7, emphasis added). David was the rich man in the story, the one with all the prestige and all the wives, and yet he had stolen the one wife of his friend, Uriah! What is more, he had covered his theft with murder.

David should have recognized himself in Nathan's story and said, "That's exactly what I did—but I stole a man's wife, so my sin is so much greater!" But he was so intent on self-justification that he magnified someone else's sin and minimized his own. To borrow the analogy that Jesus uses in Matthew 7:3-5, David actually believed the plank in his own eye belonged to someone else. We are too easily troubled by the sins of others and not troubled enough by our own.

David said that the man should pay fourfold, and God used David's own words against him. As a result of later conflict in David's family, four of his sons were killed. Furthermore, the child borne by Bathsheba also died. As Jesus said, "Do not judge, or you too will be judged. For in the same way you judge others, you will be judged, and with the measure you use, it will be measured to you" (Matthew 7:1-2).

God also said that what David had done in secret—sleeping with another man's wife—would be done to his wives in broad daylight. In fulfillment of this prophecy, David's favorite son, Absalom, later took David's wives and slept with them on a rooftop in the sight of all Israel.

What a mess!

Making the Best of an Immoral Decision

By now you are no doubt thinking, *I don't see any grace in this story, only judgment; what good is coming out of this? Where is the hope? Where is the encouragement that God will bring something good out of this mess?*

David's predicament reminds me of a situation I encountered many years ago that ultimately had a redemptive outcome. A pastor I knew had to resign from his church after having an affair. What made the news so devastating was not merely that he'd had a sexual relationship with another man's wife, but that she had also become pregnant. Remarkably, the pastor's marriage survived, but the husband of the woman who had become pregnant divorced her.

Where is the encouragement that God will bring something good out of this mess?

This tragedy was only a distant memory when one day I found myself on the phone with the man who had been born as a result of that sexual liaison. Now, thirty-five years later, he told me the story of how he had been reared by his biological mother, with help from his father and "stepmother." He had since married a Christian woman and together they were building a family and serving the Lord.

When I heard his story, I could only thank God that he often brings good out of sinful situations. At the time when our world is falling apart, we can see no possible good in the situation; but if we repent and give God time, we have no idea what he will do with the messes we've made. I wonder what God might have done in David's situation if he had immediately come clean instead of taking matters into his own hands.

If we will trust him, God will surprise us with the extent of his forgiveness and grace. He eventually used David's bad judgment for a noble purpose. Much that was lost would never be regained, but some of the past was redeemed.

The Grace of Forgiveness

After David acknowledged his sin, he wrote the beautiful words that we quoted in chapter 1: "How blessed is he whose transgression is forgiven, whose sin is covered!" (Psalm 32:1, NASB). David could never return to square one; he could not relive that decision made on the rooftop. Though the past could not be changed, it could be covered. "Though your sins are like scarlet, they shall be as white as snow; though they are red as crimson, they shall be like wool" (Isaiah 1:18).

> **If we will trust him, God will surprise us with the extent of his forgiveness and grace.**

In what surely was a moving sermon, the famous British preacher Charles Spurgeon illustrated the lengths that God will go to cover our sins:

> Man piles a mountain of sin, but God will match it, and He upheaves a loftier mountain of grace; man heaps up a still larger hill of sin, but the Lord overtops it with ten times more grace; and so the contest continues till at last the mighty God plucks up the mountains by the roots and buries man's sin beneath them as a fly might be buried beneath an Alp. Abundant sin is no barrier to the superabundant grace of God.[1]

God would not rub David's nose in the dirt. He would not constantly remind David of what he had done and how much he owed God because he had been forgiven. David would still remember his sin, but it would not be on God's mind. God says, "I have swept away your offenses like a cloud, your sins like the morning mist" (Isaiah 44:22).

God says, "I have swept away your offenses like a cloud, your sins like the morning mist."

A man was walking on a long stretch of sand beside the seashore. When he looked back, he marveled at how crooked his path was. *Just like my life,* he thought. *Every step is crooked.* Hours later, when he walked back to his lodging, he discovered that there was no trace of his footprints. The tide had come in and washed away the indentations made in the sand.

The clean, moist surface before him was a reminder that he did not have to let his past control his future. The tide had washed his tracks away and given him a second chance.

The prophet Micah put it this way: "You will again have compassion on us; you will tread our sins underfoot and hurl all our iniquities into the depths of the sea" (Micah 7:19). In other words, God throws our sins into the deep blue sea and then puts up a sign: NO FISHING.

Forgiveness is always the first blessing on the pathway of restoration.

The Gift of Joy

No doubt when David was trying to cover his sin, he was "missing God." Keep in mind that David is the same man who wrote most of the Psalms, the man who told us that he longed for God like a deer longs for water. He wanted the joy he once had to be restored. So when he confessed his sin, he added, "Let me hear joy and glad-

Forgiveness is always the first blessing on the pathway of restoration.

ness; let the bones that you have broken rejoice" (Psalm 51:8, ESV); and again, "Restore to me the joy of your salvation, and uphold me with a willing spirit" (Psalm 51:12, ESV). In the wake of his sin and its inevitable consequences, his joy was back.

Many people who commit sexual sin confess and repent of their sin, but they do not allow themselves to be joyful. They believe that, as part of their discipline, they must continue to wallow in the emotional mire caused by their sin and loss. But once David had thoroughly dealt with his sin, he could enjoy the presence of God again, an experience that always brings joy.

Please keep in mind that David's request for joy did not minimize the wrongs he had done to his family. He was not frivolously joyful as he watched his family disintegrate. If you've read the rest of his story, you know that his own personal pain was deep and lasting. But—and this is important—even when we have brought grief to ourselves and others, when we know at our very center that we have been forgiven, the sense of the presence of God returns. There is joy even in our distress.

Many people who commit sexual sin confess and repent of their sin, but they do not allow themselves to be joyful.

We must pause and think this through: David rejoiced in God's forgiveness even though the consequences of his sin continued unabated. His repentance could not bring Uriah back from the dead; all the tears he shed could never bring back Bathsheba's child or her purity. David could do nothing to forestall the awesome destruction his family would face because of his sin. Even so, he could sing again.

Why could David rejoice though he was under God's discipline? Guilt drives us to God, but once we are forgiven, it is not a part of God's discipline. Consequences are a part of God's discipline, but guilt isn't. Once the guilt is pardoned, it is gone; the conscience can be cleansed. In other words, God brings acceptance and peace to our inner world, even when our outer world is spiraling out of control.

The Gift of Solomon

As God predicted, the child Bathsheba bore to David died. But now that Bathsheba had been widowed (thanks to David's evil deed, of course), we read, "David comforted his wife, Bathsheba, and went in to her and lay with her, and she bore a son, and he called his name Solomon" (2 Samuel 12:24, ESV). In Hebrew, the name sounds like *shalom*, meaning "peace." Perhaps David thought, *This little boy will be named "peaceful."* With his family disintegrating around him, he needed some peace.

Solomon is a beautiful name, to be sure, but Nathan, the same prophet who brought David the message of judgment, said that God had a different name for the baby boy. God himself named the boy Jedidiah, which means "beloved by the LORD."

Why did God give Solomon another name? Because God had a special love for this son of David. Indeed, when Solomon was born, we read, "And the LORD loved him" (2 Samuel 12:24, ESV). So God gave Solomon a name that expressed divine favor. God made a point of saying he had set his love on this child—a child who, strictly speaking, should not have been born.

God brings acceptance and peace to our inner world, even when our outer world is spiraling out of control.

When Solomon became a man, he heard the voice of the Lord tell him that he would be given an assignment from the Almighty. He would build a temple for God, and it would be the most magnificent structure ever built until that time.

Solomon was given the opportunity to build the house of God, a privilege that had been denied to his famous father, David. Four of David's sons were killed as a result of family squabbles; but this son, born to a woman who never should have been David's wife—yes, *this* son—would be blessed.

> Solomon was given the opportunity to build the house of God, a privilege that had been denied to his famous father.

And there's more.

Solomon, the man whose birth was the product of a relationship that began in an act of adultery and resulted in a heartless murder, would write the major part of one of the books of the Bible. Solomon asked God for wisdom, and God answered beyond his wildest dreams. "He spoke three thousand proverbs," we are told, "and his songs numbered a thousand and five" (1 Kings 4:32). Although Solomon's life ended in moral and spiritual compromise, we still benefit from his wisdom when we read gems like this: "The fear of the LORD is the beginning of knowledge, but fools despise wisdom and instruction" (Proverbs 1:7).

Despite Solomon's failures and the failures of his famous father, his positive impact has endured for three thousand years. Judgment tempered by grace.

The Blessing of a Lineage

Finally, both Bathsheba and Solomon appear in the lineage of Jesus Christ. In fact, the record includes not only Bathsheba, but also Tamar and Rahab, two other women whose lives were marked by notorious sins. Tamar masqueraded as a prostitute and seduced her father-in-law, Judah, after he sinned by failing to make good on a vow. Rahab, of course,

Although Solomon's life ended in moral and spiritual compromise, we still benefit from his wisdom. was a prostitute in Jericho who aided the spies sent by Joshua. In the case of Bathsheba, Matthew says, "And David was the father of Solomon *by the wife of Uriah*" (Matthew 1:6, ESV, emphasis added), reminding us of the sinful relationship by which David took a wife who belonged to someone else. And yet these flawed individuals are listed alongside the "greats" of the Old Testament, standing as a monument to God's grace.

On a three-hour plane flight, I sat next to a well-dressed, educated, successful Hindu. We talked about Hinduism and Christianity, and the differences between the two religions. Regarding karma, he said, "If you are suffering today, it is because in a previous life you did something wrong." And he added, "Karma means that everyone gets exactly what they deserve." I replied that I was so glad that karma was wrong!

"Thanks to Jesus, we don't get what we deserve," I said. "When Jesus died on the cross, he got what he didn't deserve—namely, our sin. When we trust him, we get what we don't deserve—namely, his forgiveness and righteousness." David got the mercy he didn't deserve, and so do you and I.

First Steps

If you are in a predicament like David's, what do you do?

First, run—don't walk—to God for help, comfort, and forgiveness. Be as honest as David was in confessing your sin, and present yourself to God without self-justification or excuses. Read Psalm 51, which is David's prayer of confession. You will be astounded at the depth of his repentance and his acceptance of God's grace. Make his prayer yours.

Second, find someone who can help you, someone who can give you wise advice about what your next steps should be. You might have to reconcile with someone you have wronged or submit to the authority of the leaders of your church for further guidance and accountability.

There is more grace in God's heart than there is sin in your past.

There is more grace in God's heart than there is sin in your past. For all who are willing to submit to him, God specializes in making the best of our bad decisions. Needed grace comes only through humility and brokenness.

A Prayer

Father, cleanse me from my sin, but also deliver me from the power of my lusts. I pray that I will be free from the lure of moral impurity that enslaves me. Today I want to do whatever you ask, in order to be free from the condemnation I feel because of what I've done. Forgive me, but also free me; help me to see a path I can take to move beyond my past, and give me the confidence that all is not lost.

I am willing to do anything, either in word or deed, to try to repair the damage of my selfish choices. Lead me to people who can hold me accountable and walk with me down a better path.

5

WHEN YOU'VE MADE A BAD FINANCIAL DECISION

You didn't read the fine print

Even when the economy is strong and growing, individuals can make bad financial decisions. When the economy takes a dip and times are tough for everyone, it only intensifies the consequences of those choices. When couples disagree about finances, it can lead to more stress and more pressure on their marriage. Read these tales of two husbands, both of whom meant well, but their wives will not let them forget about the money they lost because of investments that looked good but ended badly. These letters represent multiplied thousands of others in similar predicaments.

Story #1

Several years ago, I left a very successful job to open my own business. Unfortunately, due to 9/11 and other reasons, my business failed after five years. I lost about $200,000, which was my family's savings. My wife has never forgiven me for being so irresponsible.

I have lived with this guilt and shame for years, and the money we've lost is a constant issue in our marriage. I can't trust God to help me, because I suspect I made this decision without consulting him. Every day, I am depressed over it. So do I just have to live the rest of my life reliving this failure?

Story #2

We've been married for twenty years and have young children. In the past few years, we've fallen into debt. I convinced my wife that we should invest some of our savings in what I thought was a solid investment deal. As it turned out, I lost our retirement money. Thankfully, I have a job so the bank has not had to foreclose on our house, but my wife is very angry over what happened.

Even though we are making it financially, she wants out of the marriage because she feels that I have neglected her emotionally (which is true, given that I've taken an extra job trying to make up for the money I lost). She spends hours on the Internet and is corresponding with a man she dated before we were married. She's helping him with "his issues." I think I know how this is going to end, but I feel helpless to stop it. I feel not only my own pain but also that of our children.

Bad investments often lead to bad marriages!

Facing the Issues

Recently I spoke to a real estate agent who said that not a week goes by but that she counsels people who are losing their homes to foreclosure. Often they are elderly couples who have no hope of recouping their losses. Young couples, awash with debt, are filing bankruptcy. The optimism of years gone by

The optimism of years gone by has given way to anxiety, pessimism, and despair.

has given way to anxiety, pessimism, and despair. Instead of coming together, many families are falling apart, with anger toward our government, finger-pointing at one another, and bankruptcies.

The Need for Family

Unfortunately, at a time when families should be pulling together, they are being torn apart by circumstances—often involving financial pressures. No matter how much a couple loves one another or how hardworking people might be, there are times when they overextend their spending or fall for a get-rich-quick scheme. One person who had made his share of bad investments was convinced that if he were to buy a cemetery, people would stop dying! Financial stress can drive even the most committed Christian into turmoil. And all too often, this turmoil results in divorce.

The first step toward making the best of a bad financial decision is to truthfully acknowledge the past. If there is need for forgiveness, it must be requested and granted. The two stories at the beginning of this chapter represent tens of thousands of people who did not intend to have their investments go sour. They did what they did because they firmly believed they would reap dividends, no matter how unwise the investment might look in retrospect. Sure, they may not have read the fine print; yes, they may have acted foolishly, but we've all been there at one time or another. These investors must forgive themselves and seek their spouse's forgiveness. Self-justification must end and honesty must prevail. If you have squandered some of your savings, admit it. If you ignored wise counsel, admit it. If you blew an opportunity to have invested differently, acknowledge that as well.

> **The first step toward making the best of a bad financial decision is to truthfully acknowledge the past.**

Only an attitude of honesty and confession can lay the foundation for recovery and restoration—not only of lost finances, but also of ruptured relationships. Bad financial decisions will tear a family apart only if the past is not honestly acknowledged, forgiveness is stubbornly withheld, and nothing is learned from the failure. Both the wise and the foolish make mistakes, but the wise person will learn from them and the foolish keep repeating their foolishness.

Along with acknowledgment and reconciliation of the past, there must also be a change in attitude. Chuck Swindoll has concluded that we shouldn't waste our time "concentrating and fretting over the things that can't be changed." Instead, we should "turn [our] energy to keeping the right attitude. Those things we can't do anything about shouldn't even come up in our minds."[1] Despite the failures of the past, we must begin to look at life both optimistically and realistically.

That isn't to say it's going to be easy. You might have to give up all that you own, including your car, your house, and that boat, but you can still count your blessings. Someone has said that just as a forest experiences rebirth after a fire clears out the underbrush, a financial firestorm can teach us how to do with less as it renews our faith and confidence in God.

Remember, no matter how far you've fallen or how much you've lost, you are not alone. Don't withdraw into an emotional cocoon, stewing with fear and resentment. Reach out to friends and family during difficult financial times, just as in the early days in America when neighbors helped one another get through crises. Don't let your money problems turn into personal attacks within your family. Rather than pointing fingers, couples must turn to one another and say, "We can get through this together."

> **Only an attitude of honesty and confession can lay the foundation for recovery and restoration.**

Financial meltdowns should actually bring families together instead of tearing them apart. Husbands and wives must not see one another as enemies, but must unite against their real enemies: the *devil* and *debt*!

Getting to the Heart of the Matter

As difficult as it may be to admit, most—though not all—foolish financial decisions are based at some level on greed (witness the continuing allure of get-rich-quick schemes). What is more, before most investments are made, God's counsel is neither sought nor heeded. Let's face it: Our willingness to go into debt to buy cars, appliances, vacations, and accessories is nothing less than greedy indulgence. (If you don't think so, consider that the vast majority of the world's population live their lives without *any* of those things.) These sins must be faced head-on. The Bible has many warnings about the lure of money.

No matter how far you've fallen or how much you've lost, you are not alone.

Why is money such a sensitive subject? Because it makes all the same promises that God does. It says it will sustain us in good times and bad; that it will support us when we are sick and buy us pleasure when we are well. It promises security now—and if we have enough of it, security for the rest of our lives. In other words, if we have money, we can be independent of the church, independent of our family, and (we think) even independent of God.

And therein lies the danger.

Listen to this sage advice from one who knew both abundance and lack:

> Godliness with contentment is great gain. For we brought nothing into the world, and we can take nothing out of it. But if we have food and clothing, we will be content with that. Those who want to get rich fall into temptation and a trap and into many foolish and harmful desires that plunge people into ruin and destruction. For the love of money is a root of all kinds of evil. Some people, eager for money, have wandered from the faith and pierced themselves with many griefs. (1 Timothy 6:6-10)

Why is money such a sensitive subject? Because it makes all the same promises that God does.

We are born discontented, and many die discontented. God expects us to live differently, satisfied with what we have and what we are.

Financial hard times force us to examine our motives honestly. Was our foolish decision based on a greedy desire for a windfall? Was God earnestly consulted? What warning signs were ignored in making that bad investment? It's not enough for us to be reconciled to our family members when finances have been misused; it is also necessary for us to clear our conscience with God and with others who may have been affected. Without honestly admitting our motives, we are not ready to take the next step and ask God for guidance on how to move through and out of our troubles.

Here is a promise from the Bible that is all too often ignored: "If any of you lacks wisdom, you should ask God, **Financial hard times force us to examine our motives honestly.** who gives generously to all without finding fault, and it will be given to you" (James 1:5). Just as God should have been consulted *before* the investment, he should now be consulted for wisdom in how to emerge from the failure. And it is not just wisdom we seek, but rather a total transfer of ownership. We must turn our lives over into his hands. If you are skeptical, wondering what good that would do, my response is simple: Try it and see!

Husbands should also realize that their wives often have a "sixth sense" that men frequently ignore when making financial decisions. More than once in my counseling, I've heard the wife say, "I warned him. . . . There was something **Couples should never make financial investments unless they are in *hearty* agreement.** about the investment that didn't sound right to me." When asked to explain what that "something" was, most often she couldn't articulate it; but she was right nonetheless. Couples should never make financial investments unless they are in *hearty* agreement. Good listening—patient listening—on the part of everyone is essential to agreement and communication.

Learning from the Past

God is purposeful. He has reasons for allowing our finances to slide into reverse. No doubt he has many reasons to let us struggle, but surely one of his primary goals is our spiritual growth. If we miss what God wants to teach us, we will only become cynical and begin to doubt his love and care.

Seeing God's Perspective

The first lesson is the most obvious: God wants us to learn that he is with us, not only during prosperity, but also in times of adversity. When there was a famine in the land of Canaan and Isaac was tempted to follow everyone else to Egypt, God appeared to him and said, "Do not go down to Egypt; live in the land where I tell you to live . . . and I will be with you and will bless you" (Genesis 26:2-3). God promised to bring him *through* the famine, rather than offering him escape from it.

Joseph learned a similar lesson. Clearly, God was with him when he was exalted and made second-in-command in Egypt; but we also read that God was with him when he was unjustly accused and thrown into prison (Genesis 39:2, 20-21). God is with us in prosperity and in poverty; he is with us when we can pay the mortgage and when we can't.

As we face financial pressures, either of our own making or in the economy at large, I agree with John Piper that God "intends . . . to expose hidden sin and so bring us to repentance and cleansing."[2] Only adversity can expose our false loves and keep us from hidden idolatry.

God wants us to enter into the experience of believers around the world who have known nothing but financial pressure of the worst possible kind. Most of the world struggles for its daily food; thousands—yes, *thousands*—of children die each day of malnutrition.[3] Millions of Christians live in countries where there is repression, persecution, and no support system in times of crisis.

God is with us when we can pay the mortgage and when we can't.

For most of us in America, even if we've lost the better part of our retirement income or lost our home to foreclosure, we still have food on the table and a place to sleep at night. Let us begin to empathize with and pray for our brothers and sisters who are living in squalor, with little hope of the standard of living we take for granted.

The God who told Isaac to stay in the land of famine is the same God who assures us that we can face an uncertain future with confidence and joy.

The Joy of Generosity

Here's a question I hear often: Should we continue to give to our church during tough financial times? I believe it's a mistake to revise our giving percentage downward during a recession. It is through our faithful giving, as perhaps in no other way, that we demonstrate our faith in God. Paul said that the Christians in Macedonia gave out of "extreme poverty . . . beyond their ability" (2 Corinthians 8:1-3). We should give as God has prospered us, whether that be little or much.

To clarify, I believe that we should always give a percentage of our income to the Lord. If we are struggling financially, it can be a small percentage; but financial giving reminds us that all we have belongs to God, and we should not allow our setbacks to cause us to forget the needs of others. Yes, of course, there are debts to repay and bills that demand our attention, but all we have—little or much—comes from God, "from whom all blessings flow." And if we have no income, let us give of ourselves in other ways, always remembering that God blesses those who are generous.

Paul taught that if we have the desire to give more than we can, God takes that into account. "For if the willingness is there, the gift is acceptable according to what one has, not according to what one does not have" (2 Corinthians 8:12). God, who knows our hearts, is the first to understand that sometimes our desire to give is much greater than our actual ability to give; but this much is true: Generous people are blessed by God, either monetarily or in spiritual blessings. God constantly monitors our heart attitudes, and when he finds generosity there, he rewards us with extra benefits of one kind or another. The greatest blessing to recovering from financial disaster is not to be debt-free; it is to be able to give freely to others. By a disciplined recovery from financial disaster, you can increasingly help others with a wide variety of needs, sharing the love of Christ in a tangible and personal way. This, of course, is easier said than done. To seriously curb spending

We should not allow our setbacks to cause us to forget the needs of others.

is difficult for us, especially if we have been accustomed to a rather lavish lifestyle. But tough times demand tough measures.

Nevertheless, we are not exempt from being generous because times are hard. In some countries, when times are desperate, people share the little they have with one another, even to the point of personal pain and even ruin.

Climbing Out of a Hole

Whether you've lost your job, made a bad financial decision, or simply got caught in the trap of consumerism, once you acknowledge that you have a problem and that change is necessary, there are good ways to handle a financial crisis. The steps are painful, but most often lead to a favorable result. Here is a reasonable path to follow as you seek to recover financially.

> **We are not exempt from being generous because times are hard.**

Find a Reliable Counselor

First, you must get help. Proverbs 15:22 says, "Plans fail for lack of counsel, but with many advisers they succeed." In fact, part of your problem is likely that you have attempted to live without outside help in your finances. Now that you're in crisis, that has to change.

Financial advisers come in many forms. If your situation is large scale, I recommend a seasoned investment adviser or professional financial planner. But in other situations, your pastor, a financial ministry leader, a business leader, your banker, a friend, or a family member may have the insight required to assist on your road to recovery. At the very least, such a person can serve as a sounding board, counselor, and accountability partner. It's important that your help matches your problem. Find someone with a measure of expertise in finances to guide your way.

Some churches provide a financial ministry to help in such situations. Many churches, for example, use the Crown Ministries program to help those in need.[4] Begin with prayer, and then look for an appropriate individual to help you get on the right track. There is no shame in asking for help.

Married couples should be completely open with each other on all financial issues, especially when trust has been seriously compromised. Honesty is the only way to rebuild the trust necessary for a harmonious relationship. If you want your recovery efforts to result in success, there can be no hidden accounts, secret money, or impulse spending in this process. Before creating a comeback plan, you and your spouse must know the full picture, deal with any trust issues or conflicts, and commit to necessary changes in spending while obtaining advice in changing your financial perspective.

Look for an appropriate individual to help you get on the right track. There is no shame in asking for help.

Learn to Be Content with Less
Most of the world sees Americans as very self-indulgent—and they're right. Of course, there are many poor among

us, but for the most part we're all on the bandwagon of consumerism. You may not have all the stuff your neighbor has—and, unfortunately, we too

Too often, we compare ourselves to those who have more than we do.

often compare ourselves to those who have more than we do—but our first instinct should be to see our circumstances in light of the multiplied millions of people around the world who eke out a living amid difficult work conditions, rampant disease, and gross injustice.

Imagine being free from the love of money! Paul, writing from prison, testified,

> I have learned to be content, whatever the circumstances may be. I know now how to live when things are difficult and I know how to live when things are prosperous. In general and in particular I have learned the secret of eating well or going hungry—of facing either plenty or poverty. I am ready for anything through the strength of the One who lives within me. (Philippians 4:11-13, PHI)

Solomon gave us this clear bit of insight: "Whoever loves money never has enough; whoever loves wealth is never satisfied with their income. This too is meaningless" (Ecclesiastes 5:10).

Or hear it from the lips of Jesus himself: "Beware, and be on your guard against every form of greed; for not even when one has an abundance does his life consist of his possessions" (Luke 12:15, NASB).

We seek something we do not have, even when we do not have the means to pay for it, because we are discontented with our current situation. At these times, we are left with three options: We can live *above* our means, *within* our means, or *below* our means.

God was not pleased with the Israelites who complained about the food he provided them in the desert. Their discontentment led to grumbling and dissatisfaction. In response to their lack of gratitude, he judged them. We also grieve God by our lack of gratefulness and our insistence on having not only what we *need* but also everything we want.

A financial crisis is a great opportunity to face these underlying issues.

Reduce Your Debt

When you're in a hole and want to get out, stop digging! Most financial failure is due to overextended credit. The average couple has more than $9,000 in credit-card debt. They live in a house they can't afford, and they added to their debt when they bought a car. Rather than save money for a rough patch, they assumed that the future would

We are left with three options: We can live *above* our means, *within* our means, or *below* our means.

always be as rosy as the past. When a job is lost or an investment goes sour, they have no reserves, no margin to give them options. Soon they discover that they are faced with foreclosure or bankruptcy.

We must allow financial crises to teach us about the debilitating effects of debt. It is indeed a wonder that we have raised a generation of people who cannot live within their means—and who think they *don't have to*! Early on in our marriage, my wife, Rebecca, and I learned that debts can be a huge burden; it's never as easy to pay down credit cards as you think it's going to be. If you find yourself mired in debt, I recommend that you consult an economic adviser who will help you think strategically about eliminating as much debt as possible. Even if you don't have extra money to pay down that debt, there might be moves you can make to lessen its debilitating effects.

Of course, many people believe it's okay—and even wise—to accrue debt for items that will increase in value. Conventional wisdom has long held that we should stretch to buy a house, for example, because it will leverage our investment and increase in value as the years go by. However, even this "secure" investment was shown to be risky during the recent "mortgage crisis." As I write this chapter, property values nationwide are on the decline, though the trend may reverse itself in years to come. In some instances, debt may still be

> **We must allow financial crises to teach us about the debilitating effects of debt.**

reasonable and wise, but we must be cautious, prudent, and discerning when we acquire a mortgage or add capital to a business. Too often, debt destroys, ensnares, and impoverishes.

If you find that credit cards tempt you to overspend, *destroy them*! It might be best to "pay cash as you go" for all those out-of-pocket items.

Prioritize Your Comeback Plan

Life is all about priorities, including your financial life. You likely value your home over your health club membership, and your child's education over a meal at a nice restaurant. To be specific, first list your financial needs on paper or on your computer. Without a clear assessment of your situation, it's hard to change it. As Socrates once said, "The unexamined life is not worth living." This certainly applies to changing your financial outlook. Once you know what you need to do, you can begin to develop a strategy for getting it done.

If you find that credit cards tempt you to overspend, destroy them!

One couple I spoke to recently had a combined annual income of $95,000, with both spouses working. When the husband lost his job, they were down to a single income of only $40,000. Because they had been spending nearly all of their combined income, they had to find some ways to either replace the husband's income or reduce spending.

The first step in reducing overhead is to list your monthly *recurring* expenditures. For example, you may spend $30 each month for club dues or a newspaper or magazine subscription. The more of these incidental expenses that can be reduced or eliminated, the faster you'll get back on track.

Food is a major monthly expense for most families, and thus a potential area for savings. If a family of four eats fast food three times a week, the total cost could be as high as $400 a month! That's a lot of money for food that could be offset with a little planning at home. Another common expense that can add up is cell phone service. Many families pay well over $100 monthly for their phone expenses. By simply cutting a few nonessential extras, $200 or more could be saved each month without much sacrifice.

The more incidental expenses that can be reduced or eliminated, the faster you'll get back on track.

Other expenses to examine include cable and Internet subscriptions, movie rentals and other entertainment (e.g., restaurants, sporting events), supplies for pets, ATM fees (which can add up if you're not careful), and unneeded clothing and shoe purchases.

After you've cut everything you can think of, your financial adviser can help you identify and cut expenditures that might require greater personal sacrifice. Too often, we overlook opportunities to save money because we've taken our lifestyle for granted. Desperate times call for desperate measures.

Transfer Your Emotional Burden to God

No matter what your present financial situation, make a deliberate decision today to surrender yourself and all your assets to God. This transfer of ownership will take the weight off of your shoulders and put it where it belongs—namely, in God's hands. To mark this solemn event, you might even devise a small ceremony, in which you formally renounce your ownership and your rights of control, giving them over to God. The point is to draw a figurative line in the sand and step over it, never to look back.

We must learn to trust God in the midst of our crises. Jesus was very clear that God is aware of our needs: "Therefore I tell you, do not worry about your life, what you will eat or drink; or about your body, what you will wear. . . . Look at the birds of the air; they do not sow or reap or store away in barns, and yet your heavenly Father feeds them. Are you not much more valuable than they?" (Matthew 6:25-26).

Your financial adviser can help you identify and cut expenditures that might require greater personal sacrifice.

How do we take the words of Jesus and change them from wonderful but seemingly unattainable promises into reality? How do we stop worrying and trust God in a time of bad investments and economic uncertainty?

God has taught me some lessons about trust that I want to pass along to you. Many Christians pray about their financial circumstances. They are constantly asking God to take care of this and that, but they never have peace because they have never turned the matter completely over to God. Even as they cry out in prayer, they continue to bear their burden on their own shoulders. Believe me, I've been there more times than I care to admit. But when we simply pray and don't surrender, we are actually praying in unbelief. That's why our prayers are so frantic and so repetitive. We pray, and if there is no immediate response we begin to fret and believe that prayer doesn't work.

Instead, we must genuinely commit ourselves and our assets to God. "Commit your way to the LORD; trust in him, and he will act" (Psalm 37:5, ESV). This commitment means that we take what is in our hands and place it into God's hands. If we do this in a radical act of faith, we will no longer bear the weight of our burdens.

The best biblical example of this I can think of is Potiphar, who committed all the matters of his house to Joseph. "He left all that he had in Joseph's charge, and because of him *he had no concern about anything* but the food he ate" (Genesis 39:6, ESV, emphasis added). If only we had the faith of Potiphar! All that he cared about was eating three square meals a day, because his confidence in Joseph was so complete, so total, that he had no worries. When we trust God like this, we are finally free.

We must learn to trust God in the midst of our crises.

The good news is this: God is just as ready, willing, and able to care for matters that result from our own bad decisions as he is for situations that are thrust upon us, either by others or by circumstances beyond our control. God wants us to trust him with *everything*.

The path God chooses for us might not be easy, but he walks with us all the way and lightens our load. More accurately, he carries the load for us.

Once we've committed everything to him, we still pray about our needs; but now we pray with a genuine sense of joy and praise. And if God doesn't act as quickly as we think he should, we do not fret, because we no longer need to concern ourselves with *God's* affairs! And we don't have to go to sleep at night worrying about *God's* assets!

The path God chooses for us might not be easy, but he walks with us all the way.

My best advice to you is to take time right now and commit your situation to God—the loss of your job, your uncertain future, and even your spouse and children. If you have worried all your life, this transfer of ownership will be a struggle at first. Do it anyway. "Cast all your anxiety on him because he cares for you" (1 Peter 5:7).

Surrender is a proven pathway to peace!

This chapter began with the stories of two couples whose marriages were in trouble largely because of financial mismanagement. I wasn't privy to how these situations turned out, but whether their marriages were strengthened or fell apart was determined by how they responded—whether they attempted to run away from their

God teaches us ultimate values when we are in financial need.

problems or whether they chose the more fruitful path of forgiveness, understanding, and mutual commitment.

God teaches us ultimate values when we are in financial need. And as always, he stands by to help us along the way.

If you let him, whether or not you see your money restored, your soul will experience a deeper redemption.

A Prayer

Father, I have often made decisions without consulting you. Forgive me. It is so hard to trust you during this financial crisis I am going through; I don't see any hope for the future, and yet I hope in you. As best I know how, I transfer my trust to you now; help me to see my situation as *your* situation. I no longer own anything, for all that I have is now in your hands.

Teach me the lessons you want me to learn in the midst of this crisis. Help me to make whatever sacrifices are necessary to learn the difference between what is fading and what is eternal; what is necessary and what is excess. Teach me discipline, faith, and hope. Above all, increase my understanding of how deeply you care for me.

I give you all that I am and all that I own.

6

WHEN YOU'RE IN THE WRONG VOCATION

You hate going to work

Jed came home from work one day and told his wife that he had just quit his job. He had been thinking of quitting for years, but it caught his wife by surprise. She knew he didn't like working at the lumberyard, but she thought he'd stay with it because the job market was tight. And though she loved her husband dearly, she knew he wasn't qualified for many other positions. He had worked for the same company for nearly nine years, but his boss was demanding and the work was routine and boring. So he just decided to walk away from it all, hoping for something better.

Jed's uncle had made big money in real estate, managing buildings and slowly increasing his assets by acquiring more rental properties. Jed had always believed that this was the path to the kind of success he wanted—more tolerable working conditions and, of course, more money.

At the age of forty-two, Jed thought this might be his last opportunity to make a clean break with the past and get on with what he had always dreamed he could do. But even four months later with no breakthroughs on the horizon, he still could not bring himself to admit that he was unrealistic about his abilities and the high stakes of entering a faltering real estate market. With bills mounting and no prospect for a regular income, Jed was forced to take a job he disliked even more than working at the lumberyard. He was hired to do odd jobs at a service station, for meager wages, with no benefits and virtually no opportunity for advancement. Working there was such a further blow to his pride that he could not even talk to his wife about his predicament. His job felt like a death sentence. Jed went to work each day bitter and resentful.

When you are young and healthy, you always have the option of changing vocations or climbing the ladder in your business, to find better use for your abilities and earn more money. But what happens when you have no choice, when the job market and your circumstances choose your vocation for you? What if your job takes you in one direction and your aptitudes lie in another direction? Sometimes one bad decision leads to other second-best choices.

When you are young and healthy, you always have the option of changing vocations.

This chapter is not for people who have the option to switch to a more desirable vocation. Plenty of other books have been written about how to advance your career or find the job you've always wanted. I'm writing for people who are trapped—either because of their own poor choices or by circumstances beyond their control—and who need God to redeem their career and their calling. Simply put, this chapter is for everyone who is out of options—because of age, ability, geography, obligations, or market conditions. To suggest that they change jobs to better their career is to ask the impossible. Despite how much they hate what they do, they have little choice moving forward.

This chapter is for everyone who is out of options— because of age, ability, geography, obligations, or market conditions.

In a word, I intend to give hope to anyone who feels trapped in their present employment. If that describes you, I pray this chapter will give you the encouragement to see that God is with you, even in the vocational hardships of life. Rather than have you spend your life regretting the past, God can and will make the best of your situation.

Overqualified and Underpaid

Moses, the great Old Testament leader, had excellent training, but for a long stretch of years he used none of it. After an auspicious upbringing and life in the courts of the Egyptian pharaoh, where the whole world opened up before him, he spent the next forty years condemned to herd sheep in the desert, banished to the wilderness for an act he had thought would be heroic. He went from luxury and greatness to humiliation and regret. To say that he had to downsize doesn't quite capture the magnitude of his fall. No, Moses tumbled from opulence into an abyss.

Living in the desert was one thing; being forced into a vocation he despised was another. Shepherds were an abomination to the Egyptians, whose culture Moses had inherited. Now he awakened every morning without hope that he would ever be able to change his circumstances. There he was, tending sheep and assuming he would eventually die doing what he hated. Monotony, boredom, and a predictable routine greeted him every day.

In Egypt, Moses had studied mathematics, astronomy, and chemistry, as well as hieroglyphics. He had enjoyed celebrity status and had every luxury a prosperous nation could offer. One writer speculates, "If he rode forth into the streets, it would be in a princely equipage, amid the cries of, 'Bow the knee.' If he floated on the Nile, it would be in a golden barge, amid the strains of voluptuous music."[1]

Living in the desert was one thing; being forced into a vocation he despised was another.

This child of luxury and fashion could have stayed in the palace, but he could not forget his own people, the Hebrews, and the slavery they were enduring. During a visit, he saw an Egyptian beating one of his kinsmen, so Moses killed him and hid the man's body in the sand. Not surprisingly, the deed became known. The next day, when two of his fellow Hebrews were fighting and Moses tried to intervene, they turned on him. "Who made you ruler and judge over us?" asked the man who had been in the wrong. "Are you thinking of killing me as you killed the Egyptian?" (Exodus 2:14). Moses now knew that his crime of murder was public knowledge and his kinsmen regarded him with suspicion and hostility.

What hurt most deeply was that his own people had rejected him. In the New Testament, a man named Stephen gave some additional insights: "Moses thought that his own people would realize that God was using him to rescue them, but they did not" (Acts 7:25). Moses thought his people would understand. This was an unfortunate assumption. As hundreds of people who have failed in life have had to learn, it's often presumptuous to suppose that God's people will understand.

It's often presumptuous to suppose that God's people will understand.

When Pharaoh heard what had happened, he felt betrayed by Moses, who had grown up under his tutelage, and he wanted Moses dead. Because the Israelites also held him in contempt, Moses had few options. In order to save his life, he fled to the desert. He felt betrayed by his own people; worse, he undoubtedly also felt betrayed by God, who he thought would bless him for his willingness to risk all he had for the sake of his people.

When he arrived in the desert of Midian, Moses was exhausted, so he sat down beside a well. He had a box of medals; he was qualified to be the king of Egypt; but back home his reputation was forever ruined. Undoubtedly, Pharaoh let the people know that his adopted son had become a traitor. Everywhere Moses looked, there was nothing but hot sand.

Within a matter of hours, Moses went from being served in a palace to serving others in—of all places—a desert. He had never helped water sheep before, but on his first day sitting under the blistering sun, he had his first opportunity to really serve. When the daughters of the priest of Midian came to the well, Moses protected them from rough shepherds and helped them draw water (Exodus 2:17). Though he had been trained for more prestigious responsibilities, he did whatever he could to help. The inner change was beginning to happen.

Though he had been trained for more prestigious responsibilities, he did whatever he could to help.

These women did not know that they were in the presence of greatness. When Reuel, the young women's father, asked who had helped them, all they knew was that "an Egyptian delivered us from the hand of the shepherds, and what is more, he even drew the water for us and watered the flock" (Exodus 2:19, NASB). The man who would be instantly recognized anywhere in Egypt had now withdrawn to live in obscurity and humiliation. He was invited to Reuel's home and later married Zipporah, one of the man's daughters. That sealed his vocation as a shepherd.

Circumstances, not his aptitude or abilities, dictated

Moses' career choice. His training had been for leadership, but his vocation was now doing the work of an unlettered slave. He was torn between his inner world of desires and his outer world of reality. For forty years, the most intelligent conversation he would hear at work was *baa*!

How to Turn a Job into a Calling

How do you survive emotionally when you find yourself stuck in a vocational rut, overqualified for your job but with no opportunity for advancement? How do you turn a job into a calling, to give meaning to the mundane? To be *called* to a task—*called* by God—puts significance into what might otherwise be humiliating. As we shall see, what you do is not nearly as important as your attitude in doing it.

Choose Your Attitude

In the desert, Moses had a choice to make: He could either wake up every morning angry that he had to do what he hated and resentful that he was not doing what he'd been trained for, or he could learn to actually like his daily routine. To change his attitude would be to change his life. Think of the difference it would make if Moses actually saw herding sheep not as a mundane job but as a special assignment from God. That would change everything. As poet

> **What you do is not nearly as important as your attitude in doing it.**

James Oppenheim said, "The foolish man seeks happiness in the distance; the wise man grows it under his feet."

Moses didn't know it yet, but God would use this career reversal to change Moses' perspective. Later, Moses would understand that the work God does *in* us is almost always more important than the work he does *through* us. God can use any career we have chosen, whether it is to our liking or not, to accomplish his specific work in our hearts. Whether it is beyond our abilities or beneath our abilities is not what matters; it is our attitude that is most important to him. We tend to think that our outer world is what really matters, but it is our inner world that attracts God's attention. "Unfortunately," writes Dan Miller, "the path to *doing* something often bypasses the basic questions about *being* something."[2]

Years ago, a friend gave me a copy of Viktor Frankl's book *Man's Search for Meaning*, the story of life in a concentration camp in Hitler's Germany. In it, Frankl shows that age, health, education, or cleverness did not determine who would survive the atrocities in the camp. Rather, it was attitude; only those who believed that something better was coming were able to survive the hardships. God helps us see beyond our circumstances to a much larger purpose. As one writer put it, your *attitude* determines your *altitude*!

> We tend to think that our outer world is what really matters, but it is our inner world that attracts God's attention.

Moses was now miles from Egypt, geographically as well as socially. For forty years, he did what he had formerly been taught to despise. Now this prestigious child of fame and fortune would "waste" his life doing what anyone could do.

I don't think Moses ever felt completely at home in the desert; I'm sure he often felt like the proverbial square peg in a round hole. His aptitude lay in one direction, his responsibilities in another. His training appeared wasted. When his wife bore him a son, they named him Gershom, which means "foreigner" (Exodus 2:22). Moses always thought of himself as an alien, a man without a country.

But he was at a crossroads: He could either continue with feelings of bitterness and betrayal, or get on with submitting himself to what God intended to do in him. He could nurse the wounds

His job wouldn't change; but if his attitude changed, it would transform everything.

of the past or move beyond these issues to make the best of his monotonous future. His job wouldn't change; but if his attitude changed, it would transform everything.

A friend of mine accepted a job that was offered to him but then the offer was withdrawn. As tough as it was, he accepted his disappointment as from God. He also accepted the disappointment of eventually having to accept a job far beneath his expected pay and position.

Here is a test: Can you praise God for your profession even when it isn't what you would have chosen? Can you thank God for your boss or coworkers, praying for each of them by name? Can you thank God for a job in which you are overworked and underpaid? Only when we can thank God for a vocation we despise has the shift in our attitude begun to happen.

Choose Your Employer

We don't know much about Moses' devotional life in the desert, but we do know that the only way he could find meaning in a meaningless job was to begin to see God even in setbacks and disappointments. If he could see herding sheep as a calling, then even that responsibility would have its rewards. He would find God in the ordinary, not the extraordinary. God would have to be found in the mundane.

The New Testament introduces us to a radically new perspective on how to view our vocation. During the first century, there were forty or fifty million slaves in the Roman Empire, people who had no way to cast off the injustices they endured. Whether they had good masters or bad masters, they all were locked into a system. Though slavery clearly violates the biblical concept of individual dignity and equality before God, there was nothing the slaves could do to change their circumstances. The apostle Paul encouraged them to change their attitude instead:

> Slaves, obey your earthly masters with fear and
> trembling, with a sincere heart, as you would Christ,
> not by the way of eye-service, as people-pleasers [that
> is, working only when somebody is watching], but
> as servants of Christ, doing the will of God from the
> heart, rendering service with a good will as to the

Lord and not to man, knowing that whatever good anyone does, this he will receive back from the Lord, whether he is a slave or free. (Ephesians 6:5-8, ESV)

What an explosive message this was for the slaves. They could begin to work for God rather than for man; or to put it more precisely, in serving their masters they could see themselves as serving Christ. This gave their work divine significance.

During the Middle Ages, many people believed that God was concerned only with works of a religious nature—such as saying a prayer, giving alms, or doing a good deed. Then Martin Luther came along and taught that we are all priests before God, meaning that everything we do can be pleasing to God if done for

Many people believed that God was concerned only with works of a religious nature.

his glory. Thus, a scrubwoman could glorify God by washing a floor (if she did her work as unto the Lord), whereas a pompous priest with a heart far from God would not be pleasing to God, even if dispensing the sacraments. Luther said it isn't the act, but it's the attitude of worship with which we do our work that makes the difference. Did you know that three-quarters of the people who get the most attention in the Bible never held a religious job but served God in the ordinary things of life? For example, Abraham was a shepherd, Joseph was an administrator, and Luke was a doctor. God turned their day-to-day jobs into a calling.

Meditate on this: "Whether you eat or drink, or whatever you do, do all to the glory of God" (1 Corinthians 10:31, ESV). When applied, this principle can brush away whatever stands in the way of finding satisfaction in our jobs and in life itself. Notice that we should glorify God in the ordinary things of life, like simply eating and drinking; indeed everything we do should be done for his glory. Jesus demonstrated this when he washed the disciples' feet. When he stooped to do the work of a servant or slave on behalf of his heavenly Father, he was content, satisfied that he had glorified the one he loved. There is nothing shameful about a man with a PhD flipping burgers to earn a living. Even there, working a job that seems far beneath his aptitude and training, he can still bring glory to God by a job well done.

Even working a job that seems far beneath our aptitude and training, we can still bring glory to God by a job well done.

The late Ruth Graham, wife of evangelist Billy Graham, disliked washing dishes; but she put a sign above her sink that said, "Divine Service Done Here Three Times Daily." Work can give us a platform from which to witness; but more important, work itself is the witness. We witness to God of our devotion and love.

Choose Perseverance

As far as Moses was concerned, he expected to continue his lackluster career in Midian for the rest of his life. No one there would ever be impressed with his credentials; he had nothing to do but contemplate his mistake and reflect on how badly he had been treated. On the back side of the desert, nobody cared. The years turned to decades; there were no promotions, no service awards. At best he would graduate from one flock of sheep to another. But God was there. The inner change was beginning to happen.

"Consider it pure joy," James writes, "whenever you face trials of many kinds, because you know that the testing of your faith produces perseverance. Let perseverance finish its work so that you may be mature and complete, not lacking anything" (James 1:2-4). The New Testament places a high premium on patience, endurance, and the ability to keep going even if you're in a rut that you can't get out of. Here is another piece of godly advice that comes with a promise: "Let us not grow weary of doing good, for in due season we will reap, if we do not give up" (Galatians 6:9, ESV). I admire Christians who are faithful to their calling during hard times and good. They just keep at it day after day.

"Let perseverance finish its work so that you may be mature and complete, not lacking anything."

As football players go, Walter Payton was a small man, 5'10" and 200 pounds; yet he was a league-leading rusher in the NFL. It was his responsibility to carry the football into a crowd of men who were bigger than he was, only to be thrown to the ground a few seconds later. Payton carried the ball 16,726 yards in his twelve-year career. In total, he ran with the football for more than nine miles!

Imagine carrying a football for nine miles, with every inch contested by 250-pound linebackers. Payton was thrown to the ground every 4.4 yards. That means, according to my calculations, he was thrown to the ground about 3,800 times, and often he was buried under a pile of other players. A reporter asked him, "Walter, how did you do it?" He replied, "I just kept getting up."

Blessed are those who persevere! Blessed are those who get up in the morning and go to work, knowing they will

Blessed are those who get up in the morning and go to work, knowing they will be knocked down.

be knocked down—emotionally, relationally, and psychologically—and yet keep getting up. God places high value on perseverance. There is an old Yiddish proverb that says, "He who cannot endure the bad will not live to see the good." We can endure the bad if we are willing to believe in God's care, even on the most difficult days.

Don't Trade a Dime for a Nickel

When I was a little boy, my brother talked me into trading my small dime for his big nickel. I thought I was getting a bargain because the nickel was twice as big. Just so, we often trade away that which is most valuable for that which only appears to be of greater value. Financial pressure is one of the best barometers of true character. Our integrity and sense of decency is worth far more than a high-paying career that jeopardizes our relationships and demands that we compromise what we know is right and decent. Unfortunately, we often are tempted to place the highest value in our work on the money we earn; in so doing, we too often trade dimes for nickels.

For example, thanks to recent economic hard times, counterfeiting money has now gone mainstream. The authorities say that more people than ever are using technology to counterfeit twenty-dollar bills. With these duplicates, they buy everything from pizza to a tank of gas. More people than ever are selling their integrity, their character, at bargain-basement prices. Financial hardship is a time when we should learn that our integrity is worth more than money can buy. Here is some excellent business advice: "Buy truth and do not sell it, get wisdom and instruction and understanding" (Proverbs 23:23, NASB).

Don't resort to cheating, cutting corners, or making underhanded schemes, just because money is tight. Your integrity should never be sacrificed on the altar of hardship. There are some things that are even more important than life itself—and one of those things is God's glory. No position you could ever occupy could make up for a loss of character. "Stand firm . . . be strong" (1 Corinthians 16:13). In times of crisis, your faith will sustain you.

Francis Schaeffer said that there are no big people and no little people as far as God is concerned; only consecrated and unconsecrated people. That's why our vocation isn't as important to God as it is to us. Moses had to learn that there can be fulfillment even in obscurity. Yes, even when we are asked to do a job for which we are not well suited, we can find significance if we do it for God.

Elisabeth Elliot, whose husband was killed along with four other missionaries in Ecuador, worked laboriously to break down the local language into writing during a time when there were no computers or photocopiers. Then a suitcase containing two years of work was stolen and she had to start all over from the beginning. When asked if she was angry about the theft, she said, "No, it was my worship to God, and what I did for him was lost to us, but not to God." She refused to be drawn in by the prevailing belief that you have to be rewarded in this life for all you do; she was not about to trade fleeting success for true significance.

Financial hardship is a time when we should learn that our integrity is worth more than money can buy.

What if God personally appeared to you from heaven and asked you to do for him what you are required to do when you go to work tomorrow? Would that change your attitude about your present employment? We should not see our jobs as a means of earning a living, but rather as a means to serve the God who has redeemed us.

God Sees and Knows

During the New Testament era, there was no such thing as workers' rights. There were no unions, no opportunities to redress the wrongs done to the laborers. How does one remain patient in the midst of such injustice? James warns of a coming judgment for those who exploit the poor: "Look! The wages you failed to pay the workers who mowed your fields are crying out against you. The cries of the harvesters have reached the ears of the Lord Almighty" (James 5:4).

Thankfully, James also has a word for the exploited workers: "Be patient, then, brothers and sisters, until the Lord's coming" (James 5:7). Ultimately, God is going to straighten out the injustices of the workplace. Even now "the Judge is standing at the door!" (James 5:9).

Please don't misunderstand: We should work toward justice in every situation; but so often even we in our culture are unsuccessful. So many wrongs in the marketplace will only be made right when the Judge comes. Our satisfaction for justice that is not found in this life will most assuredly be realized in the life to come.

Jesus himself modeled patience, perseverance, and faith. He did not lash out at those who crucified him, but rather left his case with the Supreme Court of the universe. He was willing to wait for the final judgment to right the wrongs. "When they hurled their insults at him, he did not retaliate; when he suffered, he made no threats. Instead, he entrusted himself to him who judges justly" (1 Peter 2:23). Only with such faith can we forgive the injustices and maintain our sanity.

What if God asked you to do for him what you are required to do when you go to work tomorrow?

Every morning before I get out of bed, I pray, "Lord, glorify yourself today at my expense." And then I ask God for the wisdom to properly handle the situations that will come my way. I've found that beginning the day right means I can end the day right as well.

God wants us to endure. When we do, we receive his help and blessing.

Choose Openness to God

Humbled in the desert, alone with the sheep, Moses had time to heal. Though he did not understand why his attempt at obedience had backfired, he would one day have a life-changing encounter with the God whose purposes now seemed so obscure. As Moses' heart opened, God became his teacher. Hidden away from the trappings of luxury and power, Moses was gradually transformed as his heart was prepared for knowing the Almighty. Eventually he would get closer to God than any other man on earth.

God used the desert to teach Moses what the palace never could have. What must have seemed to Moses to be the end of a meaningful life was actually the beginning of one of the most storied careers in human history. In the desert, he had time to remember, time to reflect, and time to pray. Then, when the time was right, he met the "God of the second chance."

God wants us to endure. When we do, we receive his help and blessing.

But let's not think that God's blessing in the desert is

automatic. If we become bitter and are not open to God's leading and direction, the desert can harden our hearts instead of softening them. Jed, whose story we read at the beginning of this chapter, believed it was God's fault that he had been denied the success others enjoyed

God used the desert to teach Moses what the palace never could have.

in their productive careers. Though he awoke every morning, went dutifully to the service station, and carried out the minimum responsibilities he had each day, his bitter attitude closed him off from seeing God in his desert experience. His bitterness spilled over and affected both his wife and his children. Those who are embittered in the desert will remain bitter, and they will not bear spiritual fruit where they are planted. To some extent, it is up to us whether we want to make the best of our situation or go from one bad decision to another that might be even worse.

Believe God for Better Days

After forty years in the desert, Moses' heart was open to the possibility of knowing God. With nothing to see east, west, north, or south, he found himself looking heavenward. Perhaps he began to realize that he was closer to God as a servant in the desert than he would have been as a ruler in the palace of Pharaoh. Moses learned that we can draw near to God even when he is silent. Faith opens the door to God's presence.

Unexpectedly, Moses encountered the burning bush and

heard the voice of the Lord calling him to a new vocation. He was to be the one who would lead his people—the people who had rejected him—out of Egypt to the Promised Land. Moses had to learn that God works even when he appears silent, even when we cannot detect his movements. "Now it came about in the course of those many days that the king of Egypt died. And the sons of Israel sighed because of the bondage, and they cried out; and their cry for help because of their bondage rose up to God" (Exodus 2:23, NASB). In the course of many days—14,600 days, give or take a few—God began to work. It took forty years, but God began to answer his people's prayers.

We can draw near to God even when he is silent. Faith opens the door to God's presence.

Of course, it's easy to trust God when the bush is burning, the waters are parting, and the mountains are shaking; it's those silent years that are discouraging. But blessed are those who do not interpret the silence of God as indifference.

It's easy to talk about living by faith when you're healthy and the boss has just promoted you. When you're happy with your work and your children are following the Lord, trust comes easily. But when you've been misunderstood and misrepresented, or when you're in a job not suited to your abilities or training—when you have medical bills and an impossible marriage partner—that's when your faith means the most to God. It's in the desert, not in the palace, that God finds out the depths of your yieldedness. It's when he is silent, not when he speaks, that your faith is most precious in his sight.

Why was Moses reluctant to go when God came calling? Most likely he was still bitter because of what had happened in Egypt forty years earlier. "If you have been burned on hot milk," a friend of mine says, "you will even blow on yogurt." Moses could not forget what had happened when he had tried to help his people forty years before. He didn't want to put himself in a position where he might be rejected again. Thankfully, he eventually said yes.

For forty years, God had Moses where he wanted him— away from the eyes of others and growing his character. Moses' calling as a shepherd was the basis for his calling as a leader who would interact with the highest echelons of Egyptian power.

You and Your Desert

In his book *48 Days to the Work You Love*, Dan Miller tells the story of a young man who described his job this way: "Antithetical to my personal and professional expectations. Unfulfilling on multiple levels: Lack of meaning and purpose; a myopic pursuit of the almighty dollar; a parasitic and never-ending voyage into the shallow waters of avarice."[3] This young man might want to change jobs, but what if he can't? How do you live in such a vocational wasteland?

It's in the desert, not in the palace, that God finds out the depths of your yieldedness.

In short, if he can see his job as a calling, he will be able to bear fruit for God even in the desert. I traveled through the Sinai Desert many years ago, and it was so refreshing to come to an oasis. We couldn't see the stream that fed it, but we knew it was there. Just so, we as Christians are called to be an oasis of refreshment, even in a work environment that is morally and spiritually arid. Yes, even in the desert we can bear fruit if we are nourished and refreshed by a hidden stream.

Visualize two men working in a vocational wasteland. One takes on the character of his surroundings and becomes bleak, with no purpose, no hope, no meaning. The other man in the same environment has hidden resources and thus cultivates an attitude of helpfulness and purpose. The contrast is evident to all who have eyes to see.

Read a description of these two men, directly from God's heart to yours:

This is what the LORD says:

"Cursed is the one who trusts in man,
who draws strength from mere flesh
    and whose heart turns away from the LORD.
That person will be like a bush in the wastelands;
    they will not see prosperity when it comes.
They will dwell in the parched places of the desert,
    in a salt land where no one lives.

"But blessed is the one who trusts in the LORD,
    whose confidence is in him.
They will be like a tree planted by the water
    that sends out its roots by the stream.

It does not fear when heat comes;
    its leaves are always green.
It has no worries in a year of drought
    and never fails to bear fruit."
      (Jeremiah 17:5-8, emphasis added)

You may work in an environment where foul language and off-color jokes are common; where coworkers undercut one another and criticize. Do you join in, or is there something different about you that demonstrates that you have roots that go down to a hidden stream? God has put you in that difficult place to be his

Even in the desert we can bear fruit if we are nourished and refreshed by a hidden stream.

witness. The workplace can actually become a platform for you to winsomely witness, because you are serving Christ. It is also the place where true character can be honed.

Three men were on their knees working with stones. When asked what they were doing, the first man said, "I am cutting and chiseling stones." The second man said, "I am earning a living," and the third man said, "I am building a cathedral." Attitude is everything.

Even the life of a shepherd can become a divine calling if we let God be God in our workaday world.

A Prayer

Father, help me to change my perspective on my employment. I pray that you will give me the grace to see that you are involved with me at work day after day. Let me see my work as your assignment for me—my calling, my opportunity to bring honor to your name.

I want to thank you that my work is difficult; thank you for helping me see that this is my calling. Teach me how to develop a root system in my vocational desert. May I be your witness wherever I find myself. May I give each one of my days to you— my job, my schedule, and my relationships. I sincerely transfer them into your hands. Thank you that you are my ultimate employer.

7

WHEN YOU'VE HURT OTHERS

Regrets you can't wish away

And now the difficult part.

It is one thing to be assured of God's forgiveness for our own mistakes, but what do we do when our bad decisions have hurt others? The short answer, of course, is that we must ask for forgiveness and seek reconciliation with the person we have wronged. Even after we have caused pain in the lives of others, hope, restoration, and healing are possible. God always takes the side of those who want to do what is right despite the cost.

Recently, while I was out of town, I decided to get a haircut. Little did I know that God was orchestrating a meeting between me and the barber, whom we'll call Susan. Yes,

I believe in divine appointments. The moment I sat down in the chair, Susan asked me what I'd been doing that day. I told her I was working on a book titled *Making the Best of a Bad Decision*, and that I was working on a chapter about making the best of a difficult marriage.

She could not believe it! She told me that she had been estranged from her husband for more than a year because he had deceived her, secretly wasting much of their income through gambling. During that year of separation, she'd had an affair with a man who was now attending the same recovery group as Susan and her husband. The man's new girlfriend was aware of the affair and had told many of her friends. Susan had called her former lover's girlfriend and asked her to be quiet about what had happened, but the conversation did not go well, and now even more people knew.

Terrified that her husband would find out about the affair, Susan lived in constant fear and depression. She couldn't sleep or even relax because of the fear that any day, at any moment, her husband might hear about what she had done. He would be furious, she said, and he was "not good at this thing called forgiveness." Susan believed this would be the end of her marriage, with huge implications for her and her two sons.

God always takes the side of those who want to do what is right despite the cost.

When she finished my haircut, she leaned against a wall in the largely empty barbershop and wept. I listened and I prayed, asking God for wisdom. Although Susan had no formal religious background, she said she believed in God and had prayed in her desperation. She thought I might be the answer to those prayers. She agreed that only God could have arranged our meeting.

What do you do if you have ruined a relationship, either because of deceit or because of false accusations?

What should she do? Quite apart from whether or not a person's spouse might discover the truth, does the adulterous mate always have a responsibility to confess? And what do you do if you have ruined a relationship, either because of deceit or because of false accusations you have made? How much should you confess, and to whom should you confess?

When to Confess

Some things are better left unconfessed. For example, don't confess the negative thoughts you've had toward your spouse, your friends, or your coworkers. Nothing is gained by bringing up matters that will only alienate a relationship rather than promote reconciliation. Negative thoughts we have about others should be confessed to God and almost always left with him. Of course, there are exceptions—such as when our anger causes us to do something wrong or hurtful.

Exercising Discretion

A woman asked me, "Should I confess to having lied under oath twenty-five years ago?" Lying under oath is a serious offense; indeed, God says that hell is filled with liars. And yet, now that twenty-five years have passed, the circumstances have changed quite drastically, and it might not be feasible to confess to the people involved. Confession to someone else might be helpful, but sometimes we just have to pray and ask God for wisdom on how to resolve such situations.

I know of an instance where a husband became truly evil, divorcing his wife, using the children as pawns, and harassing his ex-wife at every opportunity. He began a series of lawsuits against his former employer, his friends, and his beleaguered wife. In such cases, even if someone had wronged him, there would have been no reason to confess, because it would only have been used as an excuse for more evil, lawsuits, and violence. There are times—very few, however—when asking for forgiveness would only serve to justify further reprisals, so it is best to leave the matter unresolved, trusting that God will reveal the truth in the Day of Judgment.

Adultery is another matter. The act is such a violation of trust, and it directly affects the intimacy of the marriage relationship. Because such a betrayal results in so much mental and emotional baggage, it is almost always necessary that it be confessed to the person who has been wronged. Yes, Susan owed her husband the truth, just as a wayward husband would owe his wife the truth. Given the nature of the marriage bond, immorality is not just a sin against the person *with* whom it is committed, but also *against* the spouse whose trust has been violated.

> **Sometimes we just have to pray and ask God for wisdom on how to resolve such situations.**

However, I must caution you that in such a confession, we not only must take into account our ability to admit to our sins, but also consider our mate's ability to receive what we have to say. Often it is wise to arrange for a counselor to guide us in what should be said (and what should not be said). I've known instances where the husband wanted to be "totally honest" and he confessed to such things as an emotional affair with

> In confession, we must consider our mate's ability to receive what we have to say.

a coworker, lustful thoughts, or whatever. Without proper guidance, such confessions often result in ruptured relationships that seemingly cannot be repaired.

Broken promises, deceitful financial dealings, and sins of abuse and anger need to be aired in the presence of the person whom we have wronged. Even if these sins were committed long ago, those who have been offended never forget what happened.

Let me ask: How long would it take you to forget that a friend had cheated you out of, say, $5,000? A year? five years? ten years? How long do you remember that someone lied to you? Without forgiveness and reconciliation, we're likely to take those memories to the grave. Very seldom does time erase the memory of a bad deed; only forgiveness and reconciliation can free us to forget and move on.

"He could never ask for forgiveness!" an elderly woman told me recently. Her husband, now in his eighties, is dying. Their children have accused him of abusing them physically and verbally while they were growing up, but he either can't or won't admit to it, and so he stubbornly refuses to ask their forgiveness.

Only forgiveness and reconciliation can free us to forget and move on.

If he thinks that because it happened so many years ago the children should have forgotten, he is simply denying reality. Think how different it would be if he humbled himself, admitted the truth, and said to his children, "Please forgive me. I wronged you terribly."

Forgiveness and Restitution

Here's the sticking point for many people: Forgiveness and reconciliation often necessitate restitution. In the New Testament, we have the story of Zacchaeus, a tax collector who had lunch with Jesus. Zacchaeus immediately saw the implications of his newfound faith and forgiveness and said, "Look, Lord! Here and now I give half of my possessions to the poor, and if I have cheated anybody out of anything, I will pay back four times the amount" (Luke 19:8). Tax collectors in those days were notorious for graft, greed, cheating, and threats. I have no doubt that salvation was costly to this man, as he generously repaid those whom he had cheated.

A more contemporary example is that of a Christian building contractor who used inferior materials to build houses. He advertised one level of quality but delivered another. When he could no longer subdue his conscience, he faced an all-important question: "Am I willing to do whatever God requires, no matter the cost?" With a growing desire to please God, he took all of his savings, mortgaged his house, and paid back as much as he could to each of his customers. I asked him, "Was it worth it?" He replied, "It was worth every penny."

What about the person who lied on an application for worker's compensation, saying that he had been injured on the job, when the injury had actually occurred while he was hunting? Now, each month for the rest of his life, he will fraudulently receive a check. When told that he should correct this, he replied, "Do you think I'd be so stupid as to tell the truth and go to jail rather than simply accept what I did and move on?" But how can a person "move on" while continuing to receive funds based on deceit? Is it not better to be in prison with a clear conscience than in retirement knowing that each day you are displeasing God?

In my files, I have a story of a man who committed murder when he was in his twenties. He was a suspect at the time, but was never charged with the crime. He later married and had several children, and he thought he would take his secret with him to the grave. But then he became a Christian. Now, with his conscience freshly sensitized, he knew he would have to do what was right. He turned himself in to the authorities and today is serving a life sentence in prison. Nevertheless, he said,

Am I willing to do whatever God requires, no matter the cost?

God was faithful to his promise to uphold me. At
the moment of truth, though I now was a prisoner of
the law, I was set free before God for the first time in
my life. I cannot describe the feeling of that burden
completely lifted—the Lord now held his once
disobedient child in his loving arms; and true to his
promise, he did not let me fall! A wonderful peace came
over my soul, such as I had never known before. I am
now confined to a maximum-security prison, serving
time for second degree murder. But I am more free and
more at peace than at any other time in my life.[1]

Here is a man who is physically captive, but spiritually free.
Nothing is more precious than a conscience that is at peace
with God.

Steps toward Reconciliation
How desperately do you want to have a conscience that is as
clear as the blue sky?

Someone has said that we are never more like God than
when we forgive; and we are never more like humans when
we realize our need for forgiveness. We also are never more
pleasing to God than when we admit to our part in a damaged
relationship. We must be willing to take whatever steps are
necessary to bring peace where there is animosity and strife.

Nothing is more precious than a conscience that is at peace with God.

Here are some steps that will help you make the best of the pain you have caused in the life of someone else. Follow this process with a heart that is open to God.

Pray Honestly

Prayer might seem an obvious and even elementary step, but let's not take the power of God for granted. Here is a promise you can claim: "The LORD is my light and my salvation—whom shall I fear? The LORD is the stronghold of my life—of whom shall I be afraid?" (Psalm 27:1). When we want to admit to truth that will reconcile us to a person we have wronged, we must call on God and ask for his strength and wisdom.

Jesus taught that private wrongs should be handled privately, but if the matter is left unresolved, then one or two others should be invited to the reconciliation meeting. And if this larger meeting cannot effect reconciliation, then it becomes a matter for the leaders of the church to resolve. It is in this context that Jesus makes an amazing promise: "I tell you that if two of you on earth agree about anything they ask for, it will be done for them by my Father in heaven. For where two or three gather in my name, there am I with them" (Matthew 18:19-20). God's presence is especially evident when we meet to give and receive forgiveness.

> **When we want to reconcile with a person we have wronged, we must call on God and ask for his strength and wisdom.**

Enlist the Wisdom of a Counselor

For serious issues such as infidelity, it is wise to make your confession in the presence of a mediator, counselor, or pastor who can help cushion the blow and help the offended person begin the process of forgiveness. In some instances, such as when the offended person might react with violence or some other form of irrational behavior, it is absolutely necessary that confession take place in the presence of a trusted and capable third party. Another reason for bringing someone with you is the need for accountability and to serve as a witness to what was said and the response received.

One of the most difficult counseling situations in my ministry was when I was present as a wife confessed to her husband that their third child wasn't his. You can imagine the shock, the betrayal, and the unanswered questions that confession brought to the surface. The woman's tormented conscience could not endure the lies and deceit any longer; the truth had to come out, despite the consequences. I tried to persuade the husband to embrace a large dose of the grace of God and accept this child as his own. He agreed to do that initially, but long afterward I heard that their marriage was on shaky ground. I lost track of the couple, but I continued to pray that their marriage would endure this firestorm.

My point is simply that there are times when we need others present at the time of confession. When there is a confrontation that could have damaging consequences, it's always wise to take someone else with you.

Determine to Take Full Responsibility for Your Actions

Our tendency is to finesse our side of the story with the intention of blaming our actions on the wrongs done to us by others, or the wrongs that our partner or our family has done to contribute to our failure. Alcoholics can be particularly adept at blaming others for their

There are times when we need others present at the time of confession.

actions; it is always the spouse's fault, the employer's fault, the coworker's fault. An attitude of denial or blame-shifting can never bring about reconciliation. The excuse-laden request for forgiveness usually results in rejection, or at best the reconciliation is only partial.

When you seek to reconcile, approach the conversation as if the fault is 100 percent yours. Let me explain why. Suppose there is a rift between you and someone else and you are quite convinced that you are only 20 percent to blame. That means you have assessed the other person's blame at 80 percent. Your inclination is to think that the other party should come to you to repair the relationship. But let me say it clearly: You must treat your 20 percent as if it is the full 100 percent, because we are 100 percent responsible for our part, whether big or small.

If you take full responsibility for your part in the breakdown of the relationship, your confession may be a bridge over which the other person will cross and in turn ask forgiveness from you. Often our desire to make things right causes others to be touched in their spirit to reciprocate.

But—and this is important—we must be willing to take the first step, no matter how the other person responds. We must clear up our side of the mess without implicating the other person. We must treat our part (however small) as if it were the whole problem, and then we must simply commit the other person to God and not take his or her responsibility upon ourselves.

Often our desire to make things right causes others to be touched in their spirit to reciprocate.

When we confess our wrong, we should not use the little word *if.* Don't say, "*If* I have hurt you . . ." Let's not pretend that we could be wrong about our perception, when we know our guilt all too well. Rather, we should simply say, "I know I have offended you, and I have come to ask your forgiveness." Then we must specify our offense so there is no doubt about the issue being resolved. Then we can add, "I hope you will find it in your heart to forgive me."

Evaluate the Response

When we confess our wrong to someone else, what we would like to hear is, "Yes, I forgive you." But it's human nature to want to avoid saying those words; most people do not want to make a clear statement that they have granted forgiveness. More likely, they will say, "It's no big deal," or they might simply say, "Okay." Of course, they also might remain silent or say, "I can't forgive you."

Remember, sometimes people don't want to extend forgiveness, because if they forgive you, they are left with the unpleasant task of taking care of their side of the ledger. They may have used what you have done to justify their anger and spirit of revenge. To accept your apology and request for forgiveness takes the weight from their side of the scale; now they must face their own part in the offense.

If they say, "I don't know if I can forgive you," ask them to let you know when they are ready. And if they do not forgive you, at least you know that you have done what you could to take care of your part of the wrong. In that knowledge, your conscience can rest.

> **We must specify our offense so there is no doubt about the issue being resolved.**

When Reconciliation Fails

What happens when reconciliation fails? Suppose when you go to someone and humbly ask for forgiveness, you are rebuffed, shamed, and humiliated. What if your request for reconciliation is brushed aside with anger and a desire for revenge?

Or what if you confront an abuser with the evil done against you? A man in our congregation told me that he confronted his uncle, who had sexually abused him. The abuser was silent for a moment and then walked away, which is the same response most abusers have when their evil is exposed.

> **What if your request for reconciliation is brushed aside with anger and a desire for revenge?**

What do we do when others won't forgive us? Or when they refuse to acknowledge the evil they have done to us? We cannot control someone else's response. All we can do is accept responsibility for our side of the equation. Sometimes we have to accept the death of a relationship or simply leave the situation in God's hands and let him settle the score.

Accept the Death of the Relationship

We must accept the fact that there are times when a broken relationship cannot be mended. In chapter 3, I told about a deacon who divorced his wife of many years to marry his new love, to the devastation of his family relationships. His new infatuation didn't last and his new wife threw him out. Later, although he confessed his sinful choices, he had to live with the knowledge that he could not repair the relationships he had ruined.

In another instance, two Christian men decided to purchase and renovate an old house and later resell it to make a profit. One bought the house and the other, who did the renovation work, charged thousands of dollars on his personal credit card for materials and supplies. Of course, he expected to be reimbursed by his friend who had bought the house. But after the renovation was done, the house simply would not sell. The man with the high credit-card debt insisted that he be reimbursed; the man who had purchased

We cannot control someone else's response. All we can do is accept responsibility for our side of the equation.

148

the house argued that he had no money and could only repay his friend when the house sold.

The men could not be reconciled on this issue for one good reason: Each looked at the situation through his own set of lenses, and they had genuine differences regarding how the matter should be resolved.

When we have done all within our power to be reconciled, we must move on in our journey. We must remember that we, along with those estranged from us, have a date with destiny. Our struggle to connect with others gives us an opportunity to grow in the likeness of Jesus, who didn't feel the

> When we have done all within our power to be reconciled, we must move on in our journey.

need to resolve all of the issues of injustice that surrounded him, but committed his case to the ultimate Judge (1 Peter 2:21-23). His Father, he knew, would eventually weigh everything on the scales of justice.

So what do we do when we are at fault and others won't forgive us? What do we do if our apologies are interpreted as hollow expressions of self-seeking, guilt-relieving clichés? What do we do if a relationship cannot be repaired because of the evil others have done to us?

Even though at times we must accept the death of a relationship, we should never give up hope. As long as both parties are still living, there remains the possibility of at least partial reconciliation. We should constantly pray for God's blessing on the lives of those with whom we are estranged and do everything in our power to restore a civil relationship, even if former levels of trust and closeness are beyond repair.

Two missionaries who did not see eye-to-eye while serving together in South America eventually parted ways. With mistrust on both sides, and with each convinced of the rightness of his own cause, a genuine reconciliation appeared beyond reach.

Even if time does not heal all wounds, it often gives people perspective.

But even if time does not heal all wounds, it often gives people perspective. Today, these two missionaries have not only forgiven each other, they have become close friends. God might accomplish such a miracle in your life, too!

If reconciliation fails, rest in the knowledge that you have done what you could to repair the breach. Whatever is not resolved on earth will be resolved in eternity.

Believe That God Will Settle the Score

Unresolved matters must be deliberately transferred to the shoulders of Jesus Christ. He can bear what we cannot. Let our sorrow over the broken relationship remind us of our great need for God's grace; but let us not be paralyzed, thinking that our lives have come to an end. Jesus was not a failure because he didn't reconcile all people to himself before he left.

Even with the best of intentions, relationships are often left hanging with loose ends. When we have done all we can to foster reconciliation, we must believe that God will resolve these matters in his own way—perhaps in this lifetime, but most assuredly in the life to come.

We can take comfort in the knowledge that God will eventually bring all things into the light. "Therefore judge nothing before the appointed time; wait until the Lord comes. He will bring to light what is hidden in darkness and will expose the motives of the heart. At that time each will receive their praise from God" (1 Corinthians 4:5). This is a reference to the judgment seat of Christ, where all unresolved matters between believers will be adjudicated.

As for the unconverted, they will bear the full weight of their sin forever. Thus, in either case, justice shall be done; punishment will be administered according to the most meticulous standards.

It is true that in human courts, "justice delayed is justice denied." However, God never loses the evidence; he does not contaminate his findings over a period of time. That's why we can wait until the final Day of Judgment for his resolution. When we have done all we can do, we must separate ourselves

We can take comfort in the knowledge that God will eventually bring all things into the light.

from the urge to take matters into our own hands. Rather, we must defer our case to God, confident that all accounts will eventually be settled.

King David came to the end of his life without reconciling with those he had wronged. After he murdered Uriah so that he could take Bathsheba as his wife, he did receive

God's forgiveness. But his tears could not restore Bathsheba's purity, and his remorse could not bring Uriah back to life. His other wives resented Bathsheba after she moved into the palace. His sons despised him because of the hypocrisy of his moral failure.

Yet David rejoiced in God, even while knowing that he'd created a mess that would never be cleaned up. He prayed:

> Let me hear joy and gladness; let the bones you have crushed rejoice. Hide your face from my sins and blot out all my iniquity. Create in me a pure heart, O God, and renew a steadfast spirit within me. . . . Restore to me the joy of your salvation and grant me a willing spirit, to sustain me. Then I will teach transgressors your ways, so that sinners will turn back to you. (Psalm 51:8-10, 12-13)

David rejoiced in God, even while knowing that he'd created a mess that would never be cleaned up.

Words of hope for all who have blown it!

Become a Healer to All Who Need Grace

The apostle Paul writes, "If someone is caught in a sin, you who live by the Spirit should restore that person gently. But watch yourselves, or you also may be tempted" (Galatians 6:1). The Greek word for *restore* was often used to describe the process of setting a broken bone. I've never had a bone set, but I suppose that if you break your bone you don't want somebody in there with a crowbar trying to straighten things out. You want tenderness, compassion, and skill.

Emotionally speaking, many people today have broken bones, either because of their own fall, or because they were tripped by someone else. Paul would say, "Make sure to set this very, very carefully." If you've wronged someone, admit it—and not just superficially. If you can be a reconciler of others, do so with tenderness and patience.

"Blessed are the peacemakers, for they will be called children of God" (Matthew 5:9).

A Prayer

Father, help me to be willing to do whatever you require to have a conscience that is free from offense. Give me the wisdom to know what I should say, to whom it should be said, and how it should be said. Give me the humility of heart and mind to seek the help of a wise friend who can guide me through this process. Give me the assurance of your forgiveness for the decisions I have made that have hurt others; and may I, in turn, be quick to forgive.

8

HOW TO MAKE
WISE DECISIONS

Wisdom for next time

One day while vacationing with my family at Lake of the Ozarks, I was lying on my back, floating on an inflated raft, enjoying the warmth of the Missouri sun. After a few moments I opened my eyes, only to discover that my mini-raft had drifted from the dock and had turned in an unexpected direction. It took me a few minutes to reorient myself to the landmarks and to realize how far I had drifted from the spot where I had set out.

That's the way our lives often go: We come to our senses and find ourselves far away from where we started, and we wonder how we got there. How did we get ourselves into the mess we're in? Sometimes we're tempted to float through life, just hoping that our raft will end up in a good place. Thanks to the law of unintended consequences, we often find ourselves in a spot that is very different from what we had envisioned. No one plans to get divorced; no one plans to go bankrupt; no one plans to work at a meaningless job. No one plans to drift through life without a clear purpose.

Why do so many people make bad decisions? Often it is because they've bought into a prevailing lie in our culture: namely, that we should all just "follow our hearts." The Bible, however, tells us that our hearts are very deceitful. We don't intuitively know the path we should take, so we drift along from one heart impulse to another. We need a better basis than our fickle feelings to guide us to a worthy goal.

We need a better basis than our fickle feelings to guide us to a worthy goal.

But how can we make better decisions as we move forward? Yes, we know that God is there for us even in our mistakes; but think of how much better it would be to avoid those mistakes in the first place. The fact that you are reading this book is proof that God isn't finished with you yet. You still have important decisions to make, and your future can be so much better than your past. Thankfully, we can always choose to give God the broken pieces of our lives and allow him to set us on the right path again.

In this chapter, I will share some tried-and-true principles that can help us make wise decisions. Whenever I've applied these principles, I have made good choices; when I have ignored them, I've regretted the path I've chosen. It is amazing the extent to which God will work to keep us from foolish decisions if we sincerely want to do what is right and good. But we also have to gladly submit to his will and purpose.

We don't know the future, but God does. Because only he can see around corners, wisdom dictates that we should enlist his help before we embark on a new venture. God gives us a promise that he guarantees to keep: If we sincerely want to follow his will, he will give us wisdom when we encounter a fork in the road. If we ask in faith, God has guaranteed that he will answer (see James 1:5-8). But

> To ask for wisdom means that we clear the decks and sign a blank check expecting God to fill in all the details.

God will not allow us to play games with him; he will not give us wisdom if we ask for it with minds already made up. To ask for wisdom means that we clear the decks and sign a blank check expecting God to fill in all the details.

We usually don't stumble into wise decisions. I pray that the principles in this chapter will help you stay on track, so that you can look back without regret, but with satisfaction, knowing that you served God to the best of your ability.

Before I share what we should do, let's take a moment to learn what we should *not* do.

Some Don'ts

1. *Don't be duped by the path of least resistance.* The easiest path is often not the right path; the easiest path frequently

leads to regret and ruin. To be more specific, when we follow our natural inclinations, we have a tendency to veer off course very quickly. Jonah, you will remember, discovered he had enough money to board a ship going west when God had told him to go east. He thought it would be much easier to take a cruise on the Mediterranean than to preach to evil people whom he hated. If you remember the rest of story,

Easy decisions often result in the most painful consequences.

he was wrong—preaching to the Ninevites would have been easier than being swallowed by a fish. God used the storm and the fish to give Jonah a second chance, and to help him realize that the path of least resistance is often a journey to the bottom of the sea.

Easy decisions often result in the most painful consequences. Often people get married because breaking the relationship is perceived as too painful. "I knew I shouldn't have married him," a distressed young woman said to me, "but I didn't have the strength to say no after all we'd been through." Breaking the engagement seemed much harder than planning a wedding; saying no after years of courtship seemed an impossible burden and would have resulted in embarrassing questions and personal pain. Instead of doing what she knew she should, she betrayed her best instincts and went through with the wedding. She proved the proverb correct: "Marry in haste, repent at leisure." She learned that easy choices often end with hard realities; often the best path is the one that is most difficult.

The word *easy* and the word *right* seldom go together. When we go with the flow, unwilling to swim against the tide, we'll soon discover that we have to settle for a decision that was easy to make but is difficult to live with. The path of least resistance makes crooked rivers and regretful Christians.

2. *Don't sacrifice the permanent on the altar of the immediate.* Amy was a young woman who didn't particularly like school, so when she was offered a position selling clothes at a local store after high school, she said yes. Having her own job spelled independence and extravagance. But ten years later, when she was married and tired of the monotony of her job, she had neither the money nor the time to go to college. She didn't know it at the time, but by doing what seemed convenient, she lost sight of the long-range point of view. When making a decision, think beyond today to the rest of your life.

3. *Don't rush into decisions, especially in matters of great importance.* Sometimes we feel great urgency to make a decision; perhaps we want something so badly that we are willing to hurry the process. When the Bible encourages us to "wait on the Lord," it means that we should wait for the Lord to give us the guidance we seek. Of course, we should not use this as an excuse to do nothing, convincing ourselves that we are "just waiting for God" when there is much we could be doing to make our lives more productive.

"Wait on the Lord" means that we should wait for the Lord to give us the guidance we seek.

I know two men who left their employer to start their own company, intending to compete with their previous employer. Nothing wrong with that, of course. But in this case, the motive was pure greed—just the desire to make more money, and also to spite their demanding, ungrateful employer. They did not bother to consult God about their decision. They already knew they had the ability to build a strong company; they had the desire to do it, and they could see no reason why their ideas would fail. But apparently God was not impressed with their wisdom; as the Bible says, pride goes before a fall (Proverbs 16:18). Their business collapsed and they wished they had stayed with the vocation they once had.

When we impulsively rush into a decision, we can't expect to receive God's blessing.

When we impulsively rush into a decision, especially if we have wrong motives, we can't expect to receive God's blessing. Yes, if we repent and pray, God will help us right where we are. But how much better to consider a long-range perspective. Life, someone has said, is a marathon, not a hundred-yard dash.

Here is a principle I've had to learn: We must give God time to say no to the decision we are about to make. I have found that God has numerous ways of opening doors or closing them. He really wants to guide us in the right way.

4. *Don't be a fool!* A fool, as defined in the book of Proverbs, is a person who will not listen to wise counsel.

He or she does not learn from mistakes and is never open to guidance. A fool is abundantly satisfied with his own wisdom. Here is a warning: "Do not be like the horse or the mule, which have no understanding but must be controlled by bit and bridle or they will not come to you" (Psalm 32:9).

Some people prefer to go shopping for counsel; if they don't like what they hear from one person, they will go to another until someone confirms what they have already made up their mind to do. If you are looking for wisdom, be prepared to hear advice with which you may not agree.

Many stories can be told of lives squandered by people who were determined to do their own thing, disregarding the wisdom of the Bible and the wise counsel of their family and friends.

Making Wise Choices in an Age of Confusion

As I've already said, wise decisions are those we make with the end in mind. We must determine who we want to be at the end of our lives if we are to make smart decisions here and now. I had a professor in seminary who told us that we should frequently ask ourselves, "What should I do today that twenty years from now I would wish I had done?" In other words, we must look beyond the immediate to what will help us further down the road. The following principles will help us stay on the right track.

We must look beyond the immediate to what will help us further down the road.

Check Your Motives

Take the time to make sure that the motivation for your decision is what God wants rather than simply what you want. Or to put it differently, the first question we should ask is not, What will make me happy? but rather, What does God want me to do? Another question is even more basic: Am I *willing* to do what God wants me to do? I think the single most important reason that we make bad decisions is because of our stubborn refusal to submit to God. Either because of fear of what he will expect of us or because we think he will restrict us, we fool ourselves into believing that we are capable of running our own lives on our own terms.

We all have a mental image of the life we want: a happy marriage, a beautiful house, recognition for our accomplishments, a few of life's luxuries, and an early retirement. All of that must be surrendered to God. The risk, I suppose, is that our ambitions might be canceled if we honestly submit to whatever God asks. We can't say, "God, please give me a preview of what you have in mind for my life so that I can choose whether I like it or not."

We're all grateful that Jesus, in Gethsemane, did not put his own personal happiness above doing God's will. "Father, if you are willing, remove this cup from me. Nevertheless, not my will, but yours, be done" (Luke 22:42, esv). Of course, most of our decisions are neither that clear-cut nor that excruciating, but the point still stands: We must take the time to ask ourselves some hard questions about what God might want. He really does give his best to those who leave the choice with him.

Balance Your Priorities

When faced with an important decision, weigh your priorities. Take a sheet of paper and write down the pros and the cons, paying careful attention to what this decision will mean to you, your family, and your own fulfillment. The job that pays the most isn't necessarily the one that is best for you. Many a person has sacrificed what is most important for something of lesser importance. So you have to ask some hard questions: What will this decision mean for my emotional and spiritual health? What impact will it have on my family? Will I be expected to compromise my personal convictions? Am I doing this just to bolster my personal status, or is there a more noble, eternal reason why I'm making this particular choice?

The risk is that our ambitions might be canceled if we honestly submit to whatever God asks.

Whenever you can, trade success for significance. Dwight L. Moody, the founder of the church I serve, had the ambition to become the most successful salesman in the area; but he changed his mind when he heard a group of Sunday school girls pray for their dying teacher. He said that money would never tempt him again. He saw the larger picture, and that motivated him to increase his work among the poor children of Chicago—a decision that led to his becoming one of the most famous evangelists in the world. Of course, I'm not suggesting that we can all do what Moody did, but we can choose significance over success as it is most often defined.

Knowledge is important when making a decision, but the facts must be combined with wisdom. Wisdom is the ability to see beyond the pros and cons to other factors that might not be obvious just by weighing the information itself. Wisdom, as I have emphasized, comes to us from God and from the lips of wise people who cross our paths.

Surrender until You Have Personal Peace

Here is another bit of wise counsel we all can apply: "Let the peace of Christ rule in your hearts, to which indeed you were called in one body. And be thankful" (Colossians 3:15, ESV). The word *rule* means that peace is like an umpire that should control our hearts, giving us a thumbs-up or a thumbs-down on what we are doing or about to do. In all things, we should be convinced that what we are doing is right and good, and in harmony with what God wants. The peace of God sits in judgment on our lifestyles and our decisions. Sometimes we experience what might be called a "check in our spirit"; that is, a hunch that we are about to embark on a wrong path. We should listen to this prompting of the Holy Spirit, especially if we have a suspicion that something isn't right. Christians are indwelt with the Holy Spirit,

Whenever you can, trade success for significance.

who can be grieved because of our sin and missteps; the Spirit also brings peace when we obey.

We can't foresee all the consequences of our decisions, but God can. And that is why it is so important not only to consult God, but also to be quiet enough in our inner being so that we can hear the still, small voice of the Spirit if we are about to make a mistake. We've all had the experience of sensing that there is a cloud over a decision we were

In all things, we should be convinced that what we are doing is right and good, and in harmony with what God wants.

about to make. When that happens, I've learned to back off and ask, What am I missing in this decision? Women often have a more highly developed sense of intuition than men. Often they have a hunch that something is amiss, and husbands would do well to listen to what their wives have to say.

There is, of course, a danger in having inner peace alone as our guide. People have made the most bizarre decisions saying that they "had a peace about it." We can talk ourselves into a false peace; we can rationalize what we want to do, and eventually our emotions will follow the path our minds have insisted on. That's why all the principles of this chapter have to be taken together as part of the decision-making process.

Expect God to Guide You in Various Ways
God does not have a "one size fits all" policy when it comes to leading us. Rest assured that he is not playing games with us, laying out options and then standing back and saying, in effect, "I dare you to choose the right path!" He is willing to guide in different ways, but he expects our willingness

to listen and obey as part of the process. The old cliché is nonetheless true: "God gives his best to those who leave the decision with him."

Sometimes circumstances dictate what our next steps should be; at other times, people give us guidance by shar-

God does not have a "one size fits all" policy when it comes to leading us.

ing their wisdom or putting us in touch with others who become a part of our decision. Often there is a confluence of events that gives us the strong suspicion that God is putting a scenario together for us that will introduce us to new possibilities. The key is to look for God's hand of guidance in all things.

I've also discovered that God often guides me when I'm not even aware of it; I just walk through a door that seems reasonable to me, and that door opens to yet another door. Only in retrospect am I able to see how important those ordinary decisions were.

Many people have been led astray by seeking a "sign" from the Lord. Like the coed who prayed, "Lord, if he calls before 10 p.m., I'll assume I'm supposed to date him." That's simply deciding in advance a desired course of action. Others

Many people have been led astray by seeking a "sign" from the Lord.

have been greatly misled because they interpreted circumstances in a way that gave them license to do what they wanted to do. Jonah probably said to himself, "Without my even scheduling it, there's a boat that just happens to be going to Tarshish. I just happen to have enough money to pay the fare, and I just happen to be so content with my decision that I can fall asleep during a storm." And yet, we know that Jonah was actually running from God.

We're back to the bottom line: Knowing God's will is all about knowing God himself, with faith that he will lead us. Continually making the basic commitment that we are willing to do God's will must always be in the forefront of our minds.

Realize That Our Decisions Are Seldom Free from Doubt

Even after we have sought God's wisdom; even after we have gathered the facts as best we can; even after we have prayed that God would lead us according to his will, bringing us peace, there can still be a residue of doubt about the decisions we have made. Sometimes we can't distinguish doubt from fear or fear from excitement. The good news, I've discovered, is that whatever doubts I've had usually evaporate after I've crossed the line and the decision has been made.

> **Whatever doubts I've had usually evaporate after I've crossed the line and the decision has been made.**

We should be encouraged to know that even the great apostle Paul felt uncertainty at times about his decisions. He was criticized by the church in Corinth for changing his mind about coming to visit them. He wanted to visit, but didn't. So he asked them, "Was I vacillating when I wanted to do this? Do I make my plans according to the flesh, ready to say 'Yes, yes' and 'No, no' at the same time?" (2 Corinthians 1:17, ESV).

He made plans that failed, plans with good intentions that did not materialize.

Honest doubts are part of our earthy sojourn.

God's Sovereign Control

Here is a promise every Christian can claim, either before or after a decision has been made: "We know that in all things God works for the good of those who love him, who have been called according to his purpose" (Romans 8:28). This awesome promise doesn't enable us to see *why* God does what he does, nor is it a quick cure for sorrow; but it is a promise we cling to because we know that God is working for our good.

Be encouraged by the *comprehensiveness* of God's purposes. "All things" means everything works together for good. Life is haphazard, with no neat categories, but God makes them fit together. He finds a place for everything. What does he use to work for our good? He uses his Word and his people, but he also uses our foolish decisions, financial reversals, and people who work against us—"all" means *all*.

Don't misunderstand. We can't excuse our sinful decisions as fodder for God's good works; but God is greater than our mistakes and wrong choices. Paul says that all things "work together." The word in Greek is *synergism*, which derives from two words—*syn*, meaning "together," and *ergo*, meaning "to work." God works and he works things together. God sees around corners and knows the outcome in ways that you and I cannot possibly fathom; and he works everything together for our ultimate good.

When I was a boy on the farm, I loved to take things apart. My eldest brother was able to take apart a tractor motor, repair it, put it back together, and make it run again. The best I could do was take apart a clock because I was intrigued by all the little wheels. Some were going in the same direction as the hands of the clock, and others were going counterclockwise. Some were going fast and some slow. Because some of the wheels were spinning in opposite directions, it seemed as if some of the parts were working against themselves. But when I looked at the face and realized it kept time accurately, I had to admit that all the parts were working together for good.

God sees around corners and knows the outcome in ways that you and I cannot possibly fathom.

Mark my words: When you have a bad day, it may be a very good day from God's standpoint. God is working to bring about your ultimate good. Only he can do that. When he synergizes events, they fall together for good. I don't know how God takes sodium and chloride, both of which are poisonous, and puts them together to create salt, without which we could not possibly live. I don't know how God takes sin and disappointment and brings them together and makes something good out of them, but I'm convinced that he does. If you love him and are called, you're in the circle of those who benefit from this special work of God.

God is working to bring about your ultimate good. Only he can do that.

The promise of Romans 8:28 teaches that God, by his power and grace, weaves, overrides, and makes events converge in such a way that there are no permanent tragedies for believers in Christ. Conversely, for non-Christians, there are no permanent triumphs. If you don't love God, you are *not* called according to his purpose and this promise doesn't apply to you. You may exist for God's good, but you will never exist for your own ultimate good apart from God.

Follow these words and I guarantee you will make wise decisions:

> Therefore, I urge you, brothers and sisters, in view of God's mercy, to offer your bodies as a living sacrifice, holy and pleasing to God—this is your true and proper worship. Do not conform to the pattern of this world, but be transformed by the renewing of your mind.
>
> **God guides us when we surrender our rights to him and are willing to do whatever task he gives us.**
>
> Then you will be able to test and approve what God's will is—his good, pleasing and perfect will. (Romans 12:1-2)

God guides us when we surrender our rights to him and are willing to do whatever task he gives us. Meanwhile, he is greater than our bad decisions, greater than our sins, and greater than our regrets. If we love him, he is there to guide us, even if we should choose the wrong road.

A Prayer

Father, I know that the greatest obstacle to my ability to make wise decisions is my unwillingness to give myself—my future and my desires, my life—over to your care. At this moment, I make Romans 12:1-2 my personal prayer. I surrender myself to you— both my past and my future—for your control and keeping. Help me, going forward, to make decisions that bring honor to your name. I give up my desire to be the captain of my own ship, and I place you at the helm, believing you will guide me wherever you want me to go.

9

THE WORST DECISION YOU COULD POSSIBLY MAKE

When you neglect to prepare for eternity

Jesus, the master storyteller, described the career of a wealthy man who made the most disastrous decision imaginable, a decision that could not be reversed.

> The ground of a certain rich man yielded an abundant harvest. He thought to himself, "What shall I do? I have no place to store my crops."
>
> Then he said, "This is what I'll do. I will tear down my barns and build bigger ones, and there I will store my surplus grain. And I'll say to myself, 'You have plenty of grain laid up for many years. Take life easy; eat, drink and be merry.'"

But God said to him, "You fool! This very night your life will be demanded from you. Then who will get what you have prepared for yourself?"

This is how it will be with whoever stores up things for themselves but is not rich toward God. (Luke 12:16-21)

The rich man's tragic mistake is that he neglected his soul in favor of pampering his body. By placing ultimate worth on his accumulated wealth—which turned out to be only of passing value—he sold his eternal destiny at a bargain-basement price. He might have had all his physical needs and desires met, but spiritually he was disconnected.

Jesus told this story to remind us that our invisible soul—the part of us that cannot be seen—is the most important part of us. Hear it from his own lips: "Do not be afraid of those who kill the body but cannot kill the soul. Rather, be afraid of the One who can destroy both soul and body in hell" (Matthew 10:28). After the body dies, the soul goes either to heaven or to hell, a place of torment. Eventually, our bodies will be resurrected and reunited with the soul to spend eternity wherever the soul has gone. To think that this man will be conscious forever, yet separated from God, should be enough to capture our attention. He had neglected the most important part of himself in favor of what only appeared to be success.

The root of his error was that he centered his life on himself rather than on God. Six times he uses the pronoun *I*. If we add the number of times he uses other personal pronouns, the total is eleven or twelve. Let's read his statement with the emphasis he might have used: "He thought to *himself*, 'What shall *I* do? *I* have no place to store *my* crops.' Then he said, 'This is what *I'll* do. *I* will tear down *my* barns and build bigger ones, and there *I* will store *my* surplus grain. And *I'll* say to *myself*, "*You* have plenty of grain laid up for many years. Take life easy; eat, drink and be merry."'"

What did he mean by "*my* surplus grain"? Did he create the kernels of wheat and program them to grow and reproduce? Did he create the soil with the right balance of nutrients so that the plants would grow to their best ability? Did he create the sun that would shine with just the right intensity? And what about the rain?

Eventually, our bodies will be resurrected and reunited with the soul to spend eternity wherever the soul has gone.

Now let's modernize the example—which strikes a little bit closer to home. What about *my* retirement fund? *my* stocks? *my* mutual funds? *my* bank account? *my* home? *my* career? When our dependence shifts from God to our accumulated riches, we have put ourselves and our possessions in place of God. Riches are deceitful for the simple reason that they give us a false sense of security.

There is a story about a speculator caught in the California gold rush. He had stayed too long in the river bed and was caught in the snow. When he was found dead in his hut, a bag of gold was lying next to him, but it could not feed him. His money could not bring him warmth; it could not restore his depleted body back to health.

To put the matter differently: This "certain rich man" lived as if this world were the only world that mattered. He acted as if his future were in his own hands. "You have plenty of grain laid up for many years," he mused to himself. How could he be so sure? He thought his future was set and secure, but that very night he learned that no matter how tightly we grasp our wealth, it never leaves God's hands or his sovereign control.

Riches are deceitful for the simple reason that they give us a false sense of security.

That very night, the rich man's soul was *demanded* of him. This word for "demanded" in Greek was used when a person had borrowed money and now the note was due. God had given this man wealth and riches; God had given him crops he did not deserve. And now the day of accounting had arrived.

At the man's funeral, people no doubt spoke highly of his skill as a farmer and his good fortune. But he was now suffering torment in hell. Had he heard the beautiful words of praise spoken about him, it would only have added to his remorse and shame. One minute after he died, he knew that his surplus grain was gone and his future was no longer under his control. He had an overwhelming realization that his eternity was now irrevocably fixed, and his future would only become worse, not better.

A Final Plea

What makes this story told by Jesus so compelling is that the rich man had made so many good decisions. Farmers don't become wealthy without some business savvy and the ability to recognize good investment opportunities. As far as his friends were concerned, he had done everything just right and had a prosperous farm to show for it. I'm sure that many would have been willing to trade places with him. And yet in the scope of eternity, he was woefully unprepared and impoverished.

The author of the book of Hebrews asks a pointed question: "How shall we escape if we neglect such a great salvation?" (Hebrews 2:3, ESV). The answer, of course, can be stated simply: There is no escape if we neglect the pardon God offers us. The biggest mistake anyone can make is to reject God's offer of free salvation to all who believe in Jesus Christ.

One minute after he died, he knew that his surplus grain was gone and his future was no longer under his control.

Throughout this book, I've emphasized that God can make the best of our bad decisions. But once we have crossed the line from life to death, God will not reverse our foolishness. There is no blessing in hell, no redemption in the torments of eternity to come.

Here are some promises you must ponder:

- Yet to all who did receive him, to those who believed in his name, he gave the right to become children of God. (John 1:12)

- "The word is near you; it is in your mouth and in your heart," that is, the message concerning faith that we proclaim: If you declare with your mouth, "Jesus is Lord," and believe in your heart that God raised him from the dead, you will be saved. For it is with your heart that you believe and are justified, and it is with your mouth that you profess your faith and are saved. As Scripture says, "Anyone who believes in him will never be put to shame." (Romans 10:8-11)

The biggest mistake anyone can make is to reject God's offer of free salvation to all who believe in Jesus Christ.

- For it is by grace you have been saved, through faith—and this is not from yourselves, it is the gift of God—not by works, so that no one can boast. (Ephesians 2:8-9)
- The Spirit and the bride say, "Come!" And let the one who hears say, "Come!" Let the one who is thirsty come; and let the one who wishes take the free gift of the water of life. (Revelation 22:17)

The most disastrous decision you can make is to neglect what Jesus offers us: eternal life both now and forever.

If you have never received this offer, do so *now*.

A Prayer

Father, I thank you for your offer of salvation. I confess I am a sinner, unable to save myself. I now understand that church membership, living a good life, and religious rituals cannot save me; I need a Savior to forgive me and rescue me from my sin. I receive Jesus Christ as my substitute, the one who died in my place so that I can be accepted by you and forgiven. Today, I lay down my rationalizations and place all my trust in Christ, who died and rose again.

At this moment, I trust your promises and pray that you will guide me as I begin a new life as a Christ follower.

Discussion Guide

INTRODUCTION: SO YOU'VE MADE A BAD DECISION . . .

1. Do you agree that "the sum of our lives equals the sum of our decisions"? Why or why not?

2. "This is ultimately a book of *hope*." What did you find in the introduction that gives you hope as you begin to read this book?

CHAPTER 1: THE WORST DECISION EVER MADE

1. What is the worst decision you've ever made? What were the consequences of that decision? Describe how you've seen God "make the best" of your bad decision. (If you haven't yet seen redemption, do you believe God can still make something good from your mess?)

2. Which do you think is more accurate: "people change only when they see the light" or "people change only

when they feel the heat"? Why are we so reluctant to admit the truth about ourselves? Explain your answer.

3. Imagine what your life would be like without shame. Discuss both the positive and negative aspects of shame in our fallen world.

4. Why do you think John Milton calls Adam and Eve's sin "the fortunate fall"? Explain why you agree or disagree with him.

5. What hope does Romans 5:20-21 give us when it comes to our sin?

CHAPTER 2: WHEN YOU'VE CHOSEN SECOND BEST

1. Like the pregnant young woman described in this chapter, have you ever felt as if you were in a situation you couldn't get out of? What happened in your situation?

2. What is the difference between fearing success and planning to fail? When do they become one and the same?

3. Sometimes we knowingly take a wrong fork on the road of life; at other times, we just find ourselves there without being aware of any wrong decision we've made. Why can we have confidence that God stands ready to help us regardless of how we got into the predicament we're in?

4. What is the "one right choice" we can always make?

5. How did God redeem and bless the Israelites after they chose "second best"? What can we learn from their story?

6. Describe a time in your life when your foolish decision "unveiled God's finest moment."

CHAPTER 3: WHEN YOU'VE MARRIED TROUBLE

1. What is the difference between a promise and a vow?

2. Why is marriage the most sacred of all vows?

3. What was the author's advice to the couple who got married in secret at the beginning of the chapter? Explain why you agree or disagree with him.

4. What foolish vow did Joshua make in the Bible? How did God make the best of it?

5. What five myths are people prone to believe when they want out of their marriage? Comment on one or two of them and explain other ways we rationalize what we want to do.

6. Do you agree that "faithfulness is much more important than happiness"? Why or why not?

7. What is the author's basic rule for responding to unhappy relationships? How would following this rule make a difference in your relationships?

8. What three things must happen for true reconciliation to take place? (See page 63.)

CHAPTER 4: WHEN YOU'VE CROSSED A MORAL BOUNDARY

1. How is King David's downward spiral consistent with the familiar pattern followed by many who have fallen into sexual sin?

2. What steps can you take, or have you taken, to avoid temptation in your life?

3. In the long run, a seemingly easier path may turn out to be the more difficult one. How is this true in David's story? How about in your own life?

4. Give examples of people you have known who have tried to cover their sin. How were they discovered and what lessons can we learn from their experience?

5. Where is grace and redemption found in David's story? How about in your own life?

CHAPTER 5: WHEN YOU'VE MADE A BAD FINANCIAL DECISION

1. Have you ever been in a situation like the ones experienced by the two men at the beginning of this chapter? What bad financial decision have you come to regret? If you wish, feel free to share why you made this decision and what you learned from the experience.

2. What kind of attitude will lay a foundation for recovery and restoration when you are dealing with financial issues? What can you do to foster this kind of attitude?

3. What are most foolish financial decisions based on? Explain.

4. Why is money such a sensitive subject? Do you agree with the author's answer? Explain.

5. Explain how "only adversity can expose our false loves and keep us from hidden idolatry" (see page 97). How have you found this true in your own life?

6. What steps does the author recommend in order to recover from a bad financial decision?

7. What does being free from the love of money look like, according to the Bible? What does it look like in your life?

CHAPTER 6: WHEN YOU'RE IN THE WRONG VOCATION

1. Have you, like Jed, ever felt trapped in your work environment? Explain.

2. How does Moses' story fit in with this chapter's theme?

3. What questions can we ask ourselves to test our attitude about work? How can we tell when our attitude begins to change for the better?

4. What radically new perspective on work did the apostle Paul introduce in the New Testament? Do you think it is realistic? Why or why not? What steps do we need to take to apply these principles to everyday living?

5. Who do you think of when you hear the word *perseverance*? What examples of perseverance do you see in your own life?

6. For the next week, pray the following prayer each morning before you get out of bed: "Lord, glorify yourself today at my expense." Observe how God answers your prayer.

7. When is our faith most precious in God's sight? Why?

CHAPTER 7: WHEN YOU'VE HURT OTHERS

1. Discuss what you think Susan should do in her difficult situation?

2. For Zacchaeus, repentance was costly. From your own experience, how have forgiveness and reconciliation come with a price?

3. How can we make the best of the pain we've caused others? Which step do you think is the most difficult? Why?

4. When confessing to others, what one word should we never use? Why?

5. Read Psalm 51. What can we learn from David's example of repentance?

6. Why are forgiveness and reconciliation worth the cost of personal humility and honesty?

7. In practical terms, how can you become a healer to all who need grace?

CHAPTER 8: HOW TO MAKE WISE DECISIONS

1. What prevailing lies in our culture do many people believe that lead them into making bad decisions? What does the Bible say about these issues?

2. Which "Don't" in this chapter do you struggle with the most? Why? What can you do to make a positive change?

3. "Whenever you can, trade success for significance." What would that trade-off look like in your life?

4. What does the author say about seeking "signs" from the Lord? Do you agree with him? Why or why not?

5. God works all things together for the ultimate good of those who love him. What examples of this have you seen in your life? What good has come out of the sin and disappointment in your life?

6. What is the most important lesson about forgiveness you have learned that you would like to pass on to others, particularly to young people?

CHAPTER 9: THE WORST DECISION YOU COULD POSSIBLY MAKE

1. Can you see yourself in the story of the wealthy man? What was Jesus's point in telling this story?

2. What is the biggest mistake anyone could ever make?

3. Which of the promises to ponder on pages 177–178 stand out the most to you? Why?

Notes

CHAPTER 1: THE WORST DECISION EVER MADE

1. Albert Camus, *The Fall*, trans. Justin O'Brien (New York: Vintage, 1991), 81.
2. From the hymn "Calvary Covers It All," by Mrs. Walter G. Taylor, 1932. Owned by the Rodeheaver Company.
3. From the hymn "Amazing Grace," by John Newton (1725–1807).

CHAPTER 2: WHEN YOU'VE CHOSEN SECOND BEST

1. Corrie ten Boom, *The Hiding Place* (Grand Rapids: Baker, 2006), 16, 227.
2. "Let Go and Let God," a poem attributed to Lauretta P. Burns in *Protecting Those You Love in an X-Rated World* by Michele Washam and Tom Mooty (Orlando: Bridge Logos, 2007), 199.

CHAPTER 3: WHEN YOU'VE MARRIED TROUBLE

1. Lou Priolo, *Divorce: Before You Say "I Don't"* (Phillipsburg, NJ: P&R, 2007), 5–6.
2. Peter Marshall, from *John Doe, Disciple: Sermons for the Young in Spirit*, quoted in "Reflections: Classic & Contemporary Excerpts," *Christianity Today* (August 10, 1998): 72.
3. Reinhold Niebuhr, from *An Interpretation of Christian Ethics*, quoted in Christine A. Scheller, "How Far Should Forgiveness Go?" *Christianity Today* (October 22, 2010): 41.

CHAPTER 4: WHEN YOU'VE CROSSED A MORAL BOUNDARY

1. Charles H. Spurgeon, "Grace Abounding," from a sermon delivered at the Metropolitan Tabernacle in London, on March 22, 1863; The Spurgeon Archive, www.spurgeon.org/sermons/0501.htm.

CHAPTER 5: WHEN YOU'VE MADE A BAD FINANCIAL DECISION

1. Charles R. Swindoll, *Day By Day with Charles Swindoll* (Nashville: Word, 2000), 229.
2. John Piper, "What Is the Recession For?" from a sermon delivered at Bethlehem Baptist Church, Minneapolis, MN, on February 1, 2009, http://www.hopeingod.org/sermon/what-recession.
3. Anup Shah, "Today, Over 22,000 Children Died around the World," *Global Issues*, updated September 20, 2010, http://www.globalissues.org/article/715/today-over-22000-children-died-around-the-world.
4. For more information, see http://www.crown.org.

CHAPTER 6: WHEN YOU'RE IN THE WRONG VOCATION

1. F. B. Meyer, *Moses, the Servant of God* (Grand Rapids: Zondervan, 1954), 21.
2. Dan Miller, *48 Days to the Work You Love*, rev. ed. (Nashville: B&H, 2010), 1.
3. Ibid., 13.

CHAPTER 7: WHEN YOU'VE HURT OTHERS

1. John Claypool, as told to Ken Hyatt, "Freedom Behind Bars," *The Standard* (April 1999), 22–23.

About the Author

Erwin W. Lutzer is senior pastor of The Moody Church in Chicago. A graduate of Dallas Theological Seminary and Loyola University, he is the author of numerous books, including the Gold Medallion Award winner *Hitler's Cross* and the bestseller *One Minute After You Die*. He is also a teacher on radio programs heard on more than seven hundred stations throughout the United States and the world, including *Songs in the Night*, *The Moody Church Hour*, and the daily feature *Running to Win*. He and his wife, Rebecca, live in the Chicago area and have three married children and seven grandchildren.